TOWN OF WILMINGTON

ESSEX COUNTY NEW YORK

TRANSCRIBED SERIAL RECORDS

Volume 7

Emma Hinds' Scrapbook
1877-1881

Harold E. Hinds, Jr., Tina M. Didreckson
and Janet Pederson

WILLOW BEND BOOKS
2012

WILLOW BEND BOOKS
AN IMPRINT OF HERITAGE BOOKS, INC.

Books, CDs, and more—Worldwide

For our listing of thousands of titles see our website at
www.HeritageBooks.com

Published 2012 by
HERITAGE BOOKS, INC.
Publishing Division
100 Railroad Ave. #104
Westminster, Maryland 21157

Copyright © 2004 Harold E. Hinds Jr.
Tina M. Didreckson, and Janet Pederson

All rights reserved. No part of this book may be reproduced or transmitted in any form or by any means, electronic or mechanical, including photocopying, recording or by any information storage and retrieval system without written permission from the author, except for the inclusion of brief quotations in a review.

International Standard Book Numbers
Paperbound: 978-1-58549-959-5
Clothbound: 978-0-7884-9490-1

Introduction

The original scrapbook is in the possession of Merri C. Peck, Town Historian for the Town of Wilmington, New York. It is not known how it came to be part of her historian's files, but at least one other Essex County Town Historian, Janet Hall, of Keene, has a Xerox copy.

As is evident from the Hinds and Pederson essay included in this volume, the scrapbook can be attributed to Emma D. Hinds. The scrapbook may have been one of two such compilations, as not all her columns in the *Essex County Republican* are included. The scrapbook also included birth, marriage, and obit clippings, as well as published poetry.

The entries are subdivided into (1) personals, and (2) subjects. Each section is further subdivided into alphabetical listings, and chronological entries. Since the alphabetical listings in essence serve as an index, we have not further indexed this volume.

Table of Contents

Introduction

"Newspaper Columns as a Source for Family History,"   1

Alphabetical Order by Person listed   11

Listing by Event   111

Newspaper Gossip Columns As A Resource for Family History: The Case of Emma D. Hinds' (of Wilmington, Essex Co., New York) 1877-1881 Scrapbook

In the summer of 1996, when Harold Hinds, Jr., was just getting started with on-site research on his Adirondack ancestors, he first met Merri Carol Peck, Town Historian for Wilmington, New York. The Peck family was attending a local camp meeting in the early evening, so Merri could not meet with him until 9 p.m. and after. Over the course of three late night sessions, twice running well past midnight, she mentioned that a scrapbook she pulled from a stack of original Wilmington records might be of interest, as the Hinds family was mentioned in some of the clippings of gossip columns. Indeed they were: some 33 times!

Merri knew little about the origin of the scrapbook, nor who "Rupert" was, the gossip column's author and the presumed compiler of the scrapbook. Harold commented in his field notebook "Rupert is obviously a good friend of the M.E. Church and of John Hinds."

Yet the rapid perusal had also led to a mistaken deduction. The journal entry for 6 August 1996 reads, "What a day...John

Hinds ca. 1880 is a Methodist [convert from Catholicism]!" When Harold discussed this with James R. Reilly, the late Irish expert--for John Dillon Hinds was an Irish Catholic immigrant who married a Baptist preacher's daughter--he patiently stated, and then restated, that he seriously doubted that John would have converted, only to reconvert, for both he and his wife were given Catholic last rites and buried in a Catholic cemetery.

Harold stubbornly clung to his "findings," but James' patient counsel grated on him. So he asked Merri to send him a photo copy of the entire scrapbook, allowing him to more carefully analyze its entries. The reanalysis not only confirmed Jim's opinion--John hadn't converted--but also convinced Harold that this gem of a scrapbook should be abstracted for its genealogical and family history information.

Perhaps even more importantly, the sum of the tidbits populating the columns might provide multiple insights into life in a town which had no newspaper: for "Rupert's" columns appeared in a regional newspaper which otherwise did not report much on Wilmington. What follows is what he and his research assistant, Janet Pederson, learned about the value of gossip!

We first determined, based on Harold's research on John Dillon Hinds of Wilmington and his descendants, that the scrapbook had to have been created by John's daughter, Emma D. Hinds, and that she was none other than "Rupert," the *Essex County Republican* Wilmington gossip columnist and vital records recorder. The frequent mention of her father, siblings, friends (especially fellow school teachers), and relatives suggested this conclusion, as did the recording of visits by relatives, near and distant, to the John Hinds household, and as did the non-*Essex County Republican* clippings, especially regarding her mother's relations in Northwest Vermont and Quebec's Eastern Townships.

But what clinched "Rupert's" identity, is her use of "we" and "us" referring to family doings at the Hinds place, as in

"Herbert E. Hinds[her nephew]...made us a short call yesterday" [6 March 1879 column]. Some 51 entries, while never stating "Rupert's" ID, provide clues, many of which are so unambiguous as to make it abundantly clear to any Wilmington reader that "Rupert" was none other than Emma D. Hinds. Most of her readers must have known who "Rupert" was, if for no other reason than that they fed her the very substance of her gossip/reports. But pen names were a period convention, one that must have provided the reporter with a greater measure of editorial license as well.

What, then, did "Rupert" report? We subdivided Emma's reports into two broad categories: (1) Those concerning an individual or particular family, and (2) those commenting on non-personal phenomena, such as the weather, or on more general aspects of group behaviors and doings. First, we introduce those entries explicitly linked to individuals, but providing insights about people in general, and especially of life in a town with no newspaper of its own. The key social institutions of church and school were given the attention they certainly deserved and frequent entries also undoubtedly reflected the fact that Emma was a local schoolteacher, and regularly attended the M.E., or Methodist Episcopal, Church.

The appointment of schoolteachers for a current term got considerable attention. For example, we were informed that Bidney Conoboy would teach school at North Elba (5 December 1877). Local schools' closing exercises, the public demonstration that pupils have learned their lessons well, often received detailed entries. When Miss Conoboy's school closed in mid-August 1878, students gave "recitations, declamations, reading[s], and dialogues," and for Mr. Hickok's school closing in March 1881, Emma listed the subject or title of every student's performance/recitation, perhaps because her own daughter, Lillian, read "He gets drunk!" The subjects and titles of works recited, taken together, are a virtual catalogue of the period's scholastic and popular culture. We also learned that prizes and report cards were distributed, but not who did well or poorly.

The town's churches were viewed through a curious filter. Sunday sermons, or the subject of other church-related meetings, were scarcely mentioned, even for the M.E. Church. However we do learn that a typical Sunday (24 June 1880) at the M.E. Church was filled with activity: class meeting, 11:30; choir meeting, noon; Sabbath school, 1:00; preaching, 2:30; prayer meeting, 7:00.

On the occasion of the "last sermon of the conference year," for example, we only learn in the 30 March 1880 column that "Rev. E. J. McKernan preached" it. Yet, the good Reverend merited some 15 entries between July 1979 and May 1881. He preached, held revivals, participated in Sunday school picnics, officiated at funerals and marriages, *and* went fishing and "all the bites he got were on his face" (16 June 1880).

On the other hand, social occasions received far more detailed attention. Sabbath school picnics, such as that of 12 September 1878, can merit lengthy reports: where it was held; the weather that day; "Tables were set for all with an abundance of goodies, lemonade provided free;" after lunch "singing, declamations, and recitations were gone through with in a manner which done honor to all participants" (again, no comments on varying quality—evidently all the children were above average!); an assortment of games were played (e.g., croquet and baseball) and the attendees were "addressed by Mr. R. Hickok and Mr. Dennis Gorman" (but no indication one of the subjects is provided).

More detailed attention also was given to Sunday School Concerts and Christmas program. The "S.S. concert held at the M.E. church last Sabbath evening" in her 22 October 1879 column, merited a rather full report. Everyone who performed or spoke is listed together with what they did: Lillian recited, Emma sang, and others did likewise or gave declamations, read essays, rendered dialogue, or gave remarks. And, oh yes, there "was no failures."

Danger and potential harm to Wilmington's citizens was recorded. Incidents of disease and illness, crimes, fire, prostitution, and demon drink were sprinkled throughout "Rupert's" columns. Outbreaks of serious diseases such as small pox, measles, and typhoid fever are noted. But most medical entries just noted that particular individuals were ill or sick. Fairly typical is "Mrs. James Bliss is quite ill, also Mrs. Thomas Watson. We hope it is nothing serious, and that they may soon recover" (3 April 1878), and "Miss Maggie Gorman, who has been very ill for the past two weeks, is considered better" (20 April 1878). On occasion, illness was pervasive. The report of 24 November 1880 reads, "There is much sickness in town," and in early April 1878 "On account of disease prevailing at AuSable Forks the board of health has closed the school there." Emma's many entries leave the definite impression that disease and illness were much on the community's mind.

Crime statistics for Wilmington at this time undoubtedly do not exist, but Emma's columns made clear that rather minor thefts were not uncommon, and probably motivated by hunger and cold. Thefts of meal, corn, flour, honey, hens, turkeys, sheep, pork, or wood were mentioned some eight times. In two cases of theft of oats and buckwheat during the Christmas season, Emma editorialized that "Those who have plenty must expect to divide these hard times" (27 December 1878). More serious crimes appear quite rare: a fatal stabbing, but in a another town (31 December 1877); and "A base outrage upon a little girl" (26 June 1878). Perhaps the most noteworthy was a crime wave carried out by a gang of thieves operating out of a local whore house (31 December 1877). Emma didn't protest the prostitution, just the thefts! She did denounce drink. She celebrated "The tide wave of temperance" *and* sharply disapproved of the breaking of temperance laws (1 March 1878; 3 April 1878).

There appears to have been a minimal presence of institutions charged with dealing with dangers. Aside from the somewhat frequent mention of doctors, the jailing of criminals seems infrequent, although George Colby was sentenced to 10 day in jail for stealing a hat (16 April 1879), and there was no mention of any organized effort to deal with fires. Just the damage was noted, as when the house of Alpheus Perry burned to the ground. The family narrowly escaped, but "Not a garment nor anything in the house was saved" (4 July 1878).

"Rupert's" chronicling of the comings and goings of visitors to Wilmington and/or to particular, local homes exposes webs of friendship and kinship. Emma noted many, but probably not all, births, marriages, and deaths, and this is of great value to genealogists, for 1877-1881 falls before Wilmington's civil vital records begin.

But for the researcher interested in a family's web of kith and kin, and in particular which linkages in this complex are those which are maintained and nourished, gossip columns can be an indispensable resource. For example, John Hinds, Emma's father, married Sarah Galusha of Berkshire, Vermont and St. Armand, Quebec. So there was a steady stream of news reported by Emma of folks in these locales: the very first clipping in the scrapbook reported the death of Linus Leavens of Berkshire Center. Leavens was undoubtedly a friend of the Galusha family, and lived not far from Sarah's stepmother. And, as well, there was a frequent reporting of visits from Vermont and Quebec: The visit of Capt. A. L. Galusha and wife of East Franklin, Vermont is noted 25 January 1880. A.L. is Sarah Hinds' half-brother. Aunts, uncles, kissing cousins, shirt-tail cousins, nieces, nephews, friends of acquaintances left behind on former moves, visited or were remembered when newsworthy.

Equally significant to those distant kith and kin who perhaps would never come to our attention, if not chronicled, are those known relatives who never appear! Perhaps some relationships were maintained through correspondence or by news brought by other visiting relatives, but it is certain that most of Sarah Hinds' many siblings and half-siblings never were mentioned in Emma's entries. Evidence suggests they were weaker links in a very complex web of kith and kin. A Family Group Sheet, which gives relatively equal weight to all family members, is transformed into a more historically accurate and sensitive grouping where some members matter more than others.

Numerous other pieces of social history linked to specific individuals or families were recorded, and many significant details may never have been noted in print elsewhere, or in contemporary official documents. Improvements to homes, farms, and small businesses were mentioned: R.C. Lawrence, we are told, plans to repair his house in the spring (23 February 1879). The arrival or departure of people was announced: Charles Fyan would be moving to Palmer Hill sometime after 9 March 1881, and would rent his farm to Frank Joudan of the neighboring town of Jay. Major purchases were noted. Thomas Gorman had purchased 12 acres from Monroe Hall, which were near the village and border his farm (26 March 1879). And in late April 1880, Miss Electa Hays was "buying new furniture," a "suspicious" purchase (evidently Miss Electa might soon marry!)

The giving of parties, social gatherings, and special celebrations were occasionally mentioned. Charley Clark and wife gave a sugar party (16 March 1887). Mrs. L. Harley "gave a quilting last week," and this also is "suspicious" (perhaps another wedding was imminent around 28 April 1880). And "Rupert" gave us a detailed description of Mr. And Mrs. H.J. Huntington's tenth wedding anniversary celebration, including their marriage date 2 December 1868, and the fact that Mrs. Huntington's sister was Miss Low, thus giving the reader the Mrs.' Maiden name. What a lovely report to flesh out the Huntington family history!

Information about jobs, in general, and in specific, was included. In November 1879 "Wood jobs, chopping and coaling, are the chief topics of interest at present." A short-lived strike at a local iron forge was recorded. The bloomers won fifty cents more per ton (5 and 12 January 1879). Marshall Rollin, we are told, would have the mail route for next year (9 March 1881). Richard Hinds was a battery salesman (21 April 1880).

Adoptions, donations, and pensions received some attention. Mr. and Mrs. Sanford have adopted the daughter of Wm. Stevenson—it is very likely that this adoption mentioned 30 March 1880 was not recorded anywhere else! Amos Hardy had made a generous donation of $25 towards the purchase of an organ for Wilmington's M.E. Church (6 August 1879). And individuals being awarded pensions, presumably Civil War pensions, were recorded together with the amount, e.g., Mrs. Ling received a pension of about $1500 (17 August 1881). Clearly, Emma's gossip columns are a gold mine of bits and pieces of personal and family information critical to putting some flesh on a genealogical outline.

Most genealogists will skim the gossip or local column searching for those items specifically linked to their relatives. As we've indicated above, those items specifically linked to others, non-relations or acquaintances, can also reveal much about the local context of family life. When these are added to a category that most often is entirely ignored, because no specific individual or family is mentioned, an even fuller portrait of local life emerges.

In particular, weather and agriculture are noteworthy. The *Essex County Republican*, where "Rupert's" columns, appeared is located in Keeseville, near Lake Champlain, while Wilmington lies in the heart of the Adirondack's High Peaks. Keeseville's weather could be significantly different from that of Wilmington. Emma began most of her weekly or biweekly columns with a brief note on the local weather. And from these it is possible to reconstruct the seasonal weather cycle for any given period.

Take for example, the period from the fall of 1877 till the summer of 1878: frost in mid-October, snow on the mountains in early November, the river froze over in late December, snow arrived that stuck in early January only to be followed by a January thaw, then in February "plenty of snow," by late March all the snow had melted, "An early spring," summer brought forth few comments unless temps fell or there was a lack of rain.

Indeed weather comments subsided with summer, but entries on agriculture filled that void. Take 1879, for example: A late spring meant fodder was scarce, and planting was delayed. Spring farm work began in late April, but as late as 12 June a frost harmed fruit trees. The fifth of June the first potato bug appeared. The hay crop was fine and haying was underway in late July. August lacked rain. From early July through September, in most years, but not 1879, she provided scattered reports on garden crops and commercial crops. A summary of crop yields was given in September 1879: "The grain crop is an average yield. Corn below average, but better than anticipated. Potatoes good" (25 September 1879). If you combined such comments on the weather and agriculture, with the agricultural census schedules for 1850, 1855, 1860, 1865, 1870, 1875 and 1880, you would have quite a good portrait of your ancestor's farming (and most were farmers) and of general agricultural patterns.

These same U.S. and N.Y. censuses' industrial schedules can also provide a general picture of local industry. For Wilmington's most important industry, the mining and smelting of iron, these general census snapshots can be supplemented by comments in the local gossip columns. Between 2 January 1879 and 9 March 1881, Emma made some 14 entries directly commenting on Wilmington's iron works, another nine on supplying the forges with wood or charcoal fuel, and nearly 60 on the Weston family who owned the principle forges. We especially learn about when the forges were running, labor conditions and wages, the difficulty of supplying the forges with wood or charcoal fuel, and the social life of the forges' owners. Indeed, the largest number of entries for any family is that for the W.F. Westons.

We have only scratched the surface, only begun to suggest the many possibilities of using gossip columns to flesh out an individual or a family, by adding regional cultural and socio-economic contexts for these people. In particular, if the locale where your ancestors lived lacked a newspaper, regional newspapers, such as Keeseville's *Essex County Republican*, often carried only occasional news of that locale in the feature sections; but the locale's gossip column in these regional papers can offer a mother lode of information for completing Family Group Sheets *and* for fleshing them out and putting your ancestors into historical context.

Alphabetical Order by Person listed			
Name Mentioned	Date	Subject	Scrapbook Page
Allen, Mrs.	9 Mar 1881	Leaving Notch House to live in Clintonville.	19
Allen, Frank	7 Jan 1878	Manager of Notch House.	3
Allen, Frank	9 Mar 1881	From North Elba. Visiting.	19
Ames, Mrs. Daniel	29 Aug 1878	From Keeseville. She, son, and daughter visiting S.G. Williams.	6
Ames, Mrs. John	14 Jul 1880	From Clintonville. She and Miss Gracie Barney of Burlington, VT. are guests at John Hinds.	16
Amos, Mr.	10 Jul [1878]	Being visited by Mr. H. Avery and family of Wadhams Mills and Mrs. Lute Evans of Saranac Lake.	6
AuSable	n.d.	Long poem by AuSable to Winnie, who has died.	21
Avery, Mr.	26 Nov [1877]	Theft of his bee hive.	2
Avery, A.	29? Aug 1880	Visiting friends in Bloomingdale.	16
Avery, Amos	23 Feb [1879]	Granddaughter Miss Carrie Avery staying with for Winter.	8
Avery, Amos	21 Apr 1880	"Quite sick." Staying with son-in-law, Mr. Jud. Bullen of Black Brook.	15
Avery, Amos	28 Apr [1880]	"Is failing." "Has been a highly esteemed citizen of this town for a number of years."	15
Avery, Amos	29? Aug 1880	James Wilson moved into his house.	16
Avery, Miss Carrie	10 Jul [1878]	At French's Hotel in Franklin.	6

Alphabetical Order by Person listed			
Name Mentioned	Date	Subject	Scrapbook Page
Avery, Miss Carrie	23 Feb [1879]	Staying with her grandfather, Amos Avery, this Winter.	8
Avery, Miss Carrie	30 Jul 1879	From Wilmington. Working at Stevens House,	11
Avery, Miss Carrie	22 Oct 1879	Recited at M.E. Sunday School concert.	13
Avery, Miss Carrie	12 Nov [1879]	Making an extended visit to friends in Plattsburgh, Ellenburgh, and Wadhams Mills.	13
Avery, Miss Carrie	25 Jan 1880	"Has purchased a new organ."	13
Avery, Miss Carrie	26 May 1880	Very sick with measles.	15
Avery, Miss Carrie	n.d. [between 9 Mar and 6 Apr 1881]	Will teach in Black Brook, at Kilns.	19
Avery, Carry	22 Mar 1876	Acted in play at Wilmington M.E. Church.	4
Avery, Fletcher	16 Apr 1881	In town.	19
Avery, Mrs. Fletcher	1 Nov [1877]	Resident of Whallonsburgh; died.	1
Ayer, Mrs. George	24 Jun [1880]	From Black Brook. She and daughters in church.	16
Ayer, Mr. and Mrs. George	1 Jul [1879]	From AuSable Forks. Their daughter, aged 2 1/2, died of diphtheria, buried in Wilmington on 23 June	10
Avery, Mr. H. and family	10 Jul [1878]	From Wadhams Mills, visiting Mr. Amos and Sanford Avery's.	6
Avery, Henry	12 Jun 1879	From Wadhams Mills, visited by Mr. and Mrs. Wm. Mihill.	10

Alphabetical Order by Person listed			
Name Mentioned	Date	Subject	Scrapbook Page
Avery, Lucius	27 Feb 1880	Spoke at Wilmington's village school's graduation exercises.	14
Avery, Lucius	9 Mar 1881	Recited at Wilmington village school closing exercises.	19
Avery, Lucius	9 Mar 1881	Elected to committee to get dialogue books of group to raise funds via exhibition for a church organ stool and chandeliers.	19
Avery, Lute	2 Mar 1881	Appointed to committee on missions.	18
Avery, Master Luttie	25 Jun 1879	Bought at Charles Sterns' in Keeseville, a hall carpet for his mother.	10
Avery, Sanford	10 Jul [1878]	Being visited by Mr. H. Avery and family of Wadhams Mills and Mrs. Lute Evans of Saranac Lake.	6
Avery, Sanford	1 Apr [1879]	Has typhoid fever.	9
Avery, Sanford	22 Sept 1880	Flying a Garfield and Arthur flag.	[17]
Avery, Sanford	14 Oct [1880]	Elected school Trustee to replace Rollin Marshall.	[17]
Avery, Sanford	n.d. [between 9 Mar and 6 Apr 1881]	One of his sheep killed by Ira Storrs' runaway team.	19
Avery, Sanford	5 May 1881	Lost 8 sheep.	20
Avery, Mr. and Mrs. Sanford	30 Mar 1880	Have adopted the daughter of Wm. Stevenson.	14

Alphabetical Order by Person listed			
Name Mentioned	Date	Subject	Scrapbook Page
Avery, Wilber	21 Apr 1880	"Sick with pneumonia," staying at Samuel Bullen's.	15
B., S.A.	23 Dec 1877	"Our friend…from below the village."	3
Babbitt, Miss	7 Aug [1880]	From Keeseville. A guest at Amos Hardy's.	16
Baldwin	21 May 1879	Cassius Winch has moved into Baldwin house.	10
Baldwin, Master	17 Aug [1881]	With Master Torrence, both of AuSable Forks, in town buying fat cattle.	21
Baldwin, Miss. Allie	5 May 1881	From St. Armond. In town.	20
Baldwin, Frank	7 Aug [1880]	From St. Armand. He and daughter are in town.	16
Ballard, Mr.	25 Mar 1878	His "people" from Malone in town visiting friends.	4
Ballard, Miss Cora	13 Jun [1878]	Visiting friends in Wilmington, Jay, and Keeseville. Will climb Whiteface.	5
Ballard, Miss Nellie	13 Jun [1878]	Visiting friends in Wilmington, Jay, and Keeseville. Will climb Whiteface.	5
Barnard, Prof.	23 Jan [1879]	Gives concert at Black Brook.	7
Barney, Miss Gracie	14 Jul 1880	From Burlington, VT. She and Mrs. John Ames of Clintonville are guests of John Hinds.	16
Bartlett, Miss	15 May 1881	Teaching at Markhamville.	20

Alphabetical Order by Person listed			
Name Mentioned	Date	Subject	Scrapbook Page
Beardsley, Mrs.	26 Aug 1879	Lectured.	12
Beardsley, Miss Libbie	19 Apr 1881	With Mr. and Mrs. Amasa Mace of AuSable, is visiting friends in town.	19
Beardsley, Mrs. S.A.	4 Sept 1879	From Clintonville. Gave a successful lecture on the education of women.	12
Beardsley M.D., Mrs. S.A.	14 Aug [1881]	Completed her medical studies, but will locate "far away."	21
Beaudry, Rev. Mr.	15 Sept 1880	Baptized 6; 2 sprinkled, 4 immersed.	[17]
Bell, Mr.	5 May 1880	"Commenced his school in the village."	15
Bell, Mr.	12 May [1880]	"Having a full school."	15
Bell, Mr.	7 Aug [1880]	His school closes "with an exhibition." He's off to college.	16
Bell, Mrs.	15 Jan 1878	Old and very ill, she is staying with her son Wm. Bell of Wilmington.	3
Bell, Emma	27 Feb 1880	Won a spelling prize at Wilmington village school.	14
Bell, Emma	27 Feb 1880	Spoke at Wilmington's village school's graduation	14
Bell, Linnie	22 Mar 1876	Acted in play at Wilmington M.E. Church.	4
Bell, Miss Linnie	21 Feb [1880]	From Wilmington. Teaching at Hazardville.	14
Bell, Miss Linnie	13 Jan 1881	Teaching in Cooper district.	18

Alphabetical Order by Person listed			
Name Mentioned	Date	Subject	Scrapbook Page
Bell, Thurlow	30 Mar 1880	Will teach Wilmington village school during Summer.	14
Bell, Thurlow	14 Jul 1880	His school will "have a grand picnic on Wintergreen Island at the close of the season."	16
Bell, Thurlow	13 Nov [1880]	Speaker at Republican victory celebration.	[17]
Bell, Thurlow	6 Apr 1881	Has returned from his school in Keene. Now clerking for W.F. Weston.	19
Bell, W.	1 Apr [1879]	From Keene. Delivered a Greenback lecture in Wilmington.	9
Bell, W.M.	15 Sept 1880	Annual Sunday School picnic to be held in Bell's grove. Markhamville SS invited as well.	[17]
Bell, Wm.	15 Jan 1878	Lives in Wilmington, and son of Mrs. Bell.	3
Bell, Wm.	25 Apr 1878	Taking in Mr. Miles as a boarder.	5
Bell, Wm.	15 May [1878]	Chosen Superintendent of Sabbath School at Congregational Church.	5
Bell, Wm.	21 May 1879	The Sabbath School Superintendent at Wilmington's Congregational Church.	10
Bell, Wm.	9 Oct 1879	His grove site for M.E. Church Sunday School picnic.	12
Bell, William	18 Mar [1879]	At the Wilmington school meeting elected Trustee.	8

Alphabetical Order by Person listed

Name Mentioned	Date	Subject	Scrapbook Page
Benedict, Adda	31 Dec 1877	Visits Wilmington and now is Mrs. Percival Nye.	3
Benham, Mr.	5 Dec 1877	Lives in Markhamville. Mrs. Isaac Vanderwaker is his mother-in-law.	2
Benham, Sol	19 June [1878]	Moved to Markhamville and took possession of his father's farm.	5
Benway, _____	16 Apr [1879]	He and Kemp will take possession of Clinton House in AuSable Forks this month.	9
Benway, S.	23 Feb [1879]	From Frelightsburg, P.Q. Visits J. Hinds. Is negotiating to lease Clinton House in AuSable Forks	8
Bigelow, Miss	27 Jan 1881[AuSable Forks]	Teaches at AuSable Forks school.	18
Billings, Josh	13 Aug [1879]	His advice: "Don't forget to giggle."	11
Black, Mr.	n.d. [between 9 Mar and 6 Apr 1881]	Daughter quite ill with lung fever.	19
Bliss and Bosworth	26 Nov 1879	Flour and Feed store.	13
Bliss _____	4 Jul [1878]	Mill property not retained by Mr. Goodrich.	6
Bliss, Mr.	16 Dec 1878	Owns grist mill; $1000 damage in freshet.	7
Bliss, Miss	21 Jul [1881]	Village school teacher.	21
Bliss, Mrs.	26 Nov [1877]	Regaining her sight.	2

Alphabetical Order by Person listed

Name Mentioned	Date	Subject	Scrapbook Page
Bliss, Miss E.	17 Jun [1881]	Very successfully teaching village school.	20
Bliss, Ed.	26 Aug 1879	From Wilmington. At Stevens House.	12
Bliss, Edmond	26 Nov [1877]	With sister, Effie, visiting friends Seth Wardner and sister for Thanksgiving in Bloomingdale.	2
Bliss, Edmond	13 Jun [1878]	Will spend Summer at North Elba's Stephens Hotel.	5
Bliss, Edmond	14 Jul 1880	Will spend Summer in Elizabethtown.	16
Bliss, Edmond	7 Aug [1880]	Returned from Elizabethtown and is now staging for North Elba's Stevens House.	16
Bliss, Edmond	9 Mar 1881	Elected Secretary of group to raise funds via an exhibition for a church organ stool and chandeliers.	19
Bliss, Edmond	6 Apr 1881	Returned from Malone where he was visiting friends	19
Bliss, Edmond	21 Apr 1881	Purchased a fine horse of Henry Stevens of North Elba.	20
Bliss, Edmond	22 Jun [1881]	Engaged for season at Grand View House.	20
Bliss, Edmond	17 Jul 1879	Employed by J. Stevens of North Elba, who is in hotel business.	11

Alphabetical Order by Person listed			
Name Mentioned	Date	Subject	Scrapbook Page
Bliss, Effie	26 Nov [1877]	With brother, Edmond, visiting friends Seth Wardner and sister for Thanksgiving in Bloomingdale.	2
Bliss, Effie	13 Jun [1878]	Will spend Summer at North Elba's Stephens Hotel.	5
Bliss, Effie	26 Aug 1879	From Wilmington. At Stevens House.	12
Bliss, Effie	25 Jan 1880	Is ill.	13
Bliss, Effie	9 Mar 1881	Elected to committee to get Dialogue Books of group to raise funds via exhibition for a church organ stool and chandeliers.	19
Bliss, Effie M.	22 Oct 1877	Sabbath School recital.	1
Bliss, Effie M.	22 Mar 1878	Acted in play at Wilmington M.E. Church.	4
Bliss, Miss Effie	12 Mar 1879	Has returned to North Elba.	8
Bliss, Miss Effie	30 Apr [1879]	Home from North Elba. Will teach the young how to shoot this Summer.	9
Bliss, Miss Effie	6 Aug [1879]	Her school will close. She's off to Stevens House.	11
Bliss, Miss Effie	22 Oct 1879	Sang at M.E. Sunday School concert.	13
Bliss, Miss Effie	26 Nov 1879	Teaching at "Rogers Kilns on the mountain."	13
Bliss, Miss Effie	27 Feb 1880	Considering purchasing an organ.	14

Alphabetical Order by Person listed			
Name Mentioned	Date	Subject	Scrapbook Page
Bliss, Miss Effie	30 Mar 1880	Will teach "on the mountain at Roger's Kilns."	14
Bliss, Miss Effie	23 Dec 1880	Will teach at "the upper forge."	[17]
Bliss, Miss Effie	16 Feb [1881]	Her school closed, and now she's attending the village school.	18
Bliss, Miss Effie	9 Mar 1881	Recited at Wilmington school exercises.	19
Bliss, Miss Effie	9 Mar 1881	Purchased a sewing machine.	19
Bliss, Miss Effie	n.d. [between 9 Mar and 6 Apr 1881]	Will teach at village school, from mid-April.	19
Bliss, Miss Effie	22 Jun [1881]	Received a specimen box of Colorado minerals, as did Miss Mary Gorman, from the brothers Thomas Jr. and Mike Gorman in Colorado.	20
Bliss, Miss Effie	4 Aug 1881	"Gone to Lake Placid."	21
Bliss, Flora C.	Marriage, n.d.	Married Theodore H. White 6 Aug 1878 at Wilmington's Congregational Parsonage by Rev. T. Watson. Bride resides in Wilmington.	5
Bliss, Frank	27 Dec [1878]	Lost a cow.	7
Bliss, Frank	26 Aug 1879	From Wilmington. At Stevens House.	12
Bliss, Iva	14 Aug 1878	Reads paper at school's closing exercises.	6

Alphabetical Order by Person listed			
Name Mentioned	Date	Subject	Scrapbook Page
Bliss, Iva	21 Jul [1881]	Recites at village school closing ceremonies.	21
Bliss, Miss Iva	9 Mar 1881	Recited at Wilmington village school closing exercises.	19
Bliss, J.	22 Oct 1877	Sabbath School recital.	1
Bliss, James	21 May [1878]	Chosen Superintendent of Wilmington M.E. Church Sabbath School.	5
Bliss, James	19 June [1878]	Sold grist mill property for $5000.	5
Bliss, James	24 Aug 1878	Has hired someone from Sandy Hill to repair his grist mill	6
Bliss, James	16 Dec 1878	Employed Mr. Hoxie of Sandy Hill to repair grist	7
Bliss, James	12 Feb 1879	Theft of flour from his grist mill.	8
Bliss, James	21 May 1879	The Sabbath School Superintendent at M.E Church.	10
Bliss, James	6 Aug [1879]	"Has taken his team to North Elba, and is staging for J. Stevens"	11
Bliss, James	26 Aug 1879	From Wilmington. At Stevens House.	12
Bliss, James	9 Oct 1879	Spoke at M. E. Church Sunday School picnic.	12
Bliss, James	22 Oct 1879	Conducted speaking at M. E. Church Sunday School concert.	13
Bliss, James	22 Oct 1879	Elected Trustee at annual school meeting for two year term.	13
Bliss, James	21 Apr 1880	Seriously ill with "inflammatory rheumatism."	15

Alphabetical Order by Person listed

Name Mentioned	Date	Subject	Scrapbook Page
Bliss, James	28 Apr [1880]	"Dangerously ill."	15
Bliss, James	5 May 1880	"Is recovering."	15
Bliss, James	14 Jul 1880	Recovering slowly.	16
Bliss, Mrs. James	3 Apr 1878	Quite ill.	4
Bliss, Mrs. James	20 Apr 1878	"Slowly recovering."	4
Bliss, Mrs. James	9 Mar 1881	Mrs. Joseph Bliss, her mother, bought a sewing machine for her.	19
Bliss, Jas	2 Jan [1879]	His grist mill is operating again.	7
Bliss, Jasper	20 Nov [1877]	Victim of theft.	1
Bliss, Jasper	25 Apr 1878	Remodeling his house and grounds.	5
Bliss, Jasper	12 Mar 1879	His daughter, Mrs. Fuller of Mechum Lake, in Wilmington visiting friends.	8
Bliss, Jasper	16 Apr [1879]	Mrs. Hart of Keeseville is removing his two facial cancers	9
Bliss, Jasper	14 Jul 1880	He "bid off" the town house.	16
Bliss, Mrs. Jasper	1 Nov [1877]	Has become blind.	1
Bliss, Mrs. Joseph	9 Mar 1881	Ordered a sewing machine "as a gift to her daughter, Mrs. James Bliss."	19
Bliss, L.	22 Oct 1877	Sabbath School recital.	1
Bliss, L.	15 Sept 1880	Henry Lamoy has moved into upper part of his house.	[17]

Alphabetical Order by Person listed			
Name Mentioned	Date	Subject	Scrapbook Page
Bliss, Mr. L.	19 Apr 1881	Went fishing with Mr. W.F. Weston up the river. "Not a bite."	19
Bliss, Loami	n.d. (between 9 Mar and 6 Apr 1881)	Lost two yearlings to the "murain."	19
Bliss, Loami	17 Aug [1881]	Miss Lillie Macomber and friends of Clintonville were guests of.	21
Bliss, Mr. Loami	26 Nov [1877]	Remodeling house.	2
Bliss, Mr. Loami	9 Mar 1881	Mrs. Fletcher of North Elba is his guest.	19
Bliss, Loamie	13 Jun [1878]	Lost a valuable horse.	5
Bliss, Loamie	2 Mar 1881	Mr. and Mrs. Henry Stevens and son of Burlington, VT were guests at.	18
Bliss, Mrs. Loammi	16 Apr [1879]	She and son visiting friends in Clintonville.	9
Bliss, Mr. and Mrs. Loammi	24 Apr 1879	Visited friends in Port Jackson. Report of 16 Apr incorrect.	9
Blood, Mr.	20 Nov [1877]	Grew a large pumpkin.	1
Blood, Mr.	25 Apr 1878	Fixing fence.	5
Blood, S.	13 Jan 1881	Spending a few days with his son in Black Brook.	18
Blood, Mr. S.	26 Mar 1879	Severely sprained his ankle.	9
Bond, Rev. J.H.	21 Feb [1880]	From Willsborough. Will lecture at Wilmington M.E. Church.	14

Alphabetical Order by Person listed			
Name Mentioned	Date	Subject	Scrapbook Page
Bosworth, Mrs.	8 Jul 1880	Her sister from Schuyler Falls, Miss Winters, visiting.	16
Bosworth, David	24 Aug 1878	From Mooers; James Bliss hires to run his grist-mill.	6
Bosworth, David	6 Apr 1881	His sister badly hurt in fall, but recovering and will return home.	19
Bosworth, Mr. And Mrs. David	Births, n.d.	A daughter born to 3 Dec 1879 in Wilmington.	11
Bosworth, Mr. And Mrs. David	22 Sept 1880	Have guests from Schuyler Falls.	[17]
Bowen, Patience	Obit, n.d.	Daughter of Straten Bowen d. 11 Jun 1878 of measles in Wilmington.	4
Bradford, Rev.	5 May 1880	From Upper Jay. Gave a discourse.	15
Bradford, Rev. C.A.	Obit, n.d.	Will preside at John S. Hinds' funeral at Wilmington's M.E. Church.	10
Bradford, Rev. C.A.	25 Sept 1879	With Rev. E.J. McKernan officiated at quarterly meeting.	12
Bradford, Rev. C.A.	Deaths, n.d.	Officiating clergyman at funeral held at Adirondack House on Sat. for Roy, son of Mr. and Mrs. E.S. Kemp, who died 14 May 1880.	15
Bragdon, Charles Rev.	13 Nov [1880]	Officiated at funeral for Mrs. Kemp, mother of E.S. Kemp, at AuSable Forks Episcopal Church.	[17]

Alphabetical Order by Person listed			
Name Mentioned	Date	Subject	Scrapbook Page
Bretell, Mr. and Mrs. Josh	Births, n.d.	A daughter born to 20 Aug 1879 in Wilmington.	11
Brewster, Byron R.	Marriage n.d.	From North Elba. Married Bidney Conerboy of Wilmington 19 Mar 1879 at AuSable Forks American House by Rev. B. Merrill.	8
Bruce, Mr.	15 May 1881	Moved into house previously occupied by C. Winch.	20
Bullen, Mr. Jud.	21 Apr 1880	From Black Brook. Son-in-law of Amos Avery.	15
Chase, Eugene	5 Dec 1877	From Vermont, visiting.	2
Child, Mrs. L.B.	26 Jun 1878	From Ogdensburgh. Theft of her Wilmington house's wood shed.	6
Child, Mrs. Laura B.	Death, n.d.	Aged 70. Died 12 Apr 1879 of paralysis in Wilmington. Her son is Dr. N.N. Child.	8
Child, Mrs. Laura B.	20 Apr 1878	Lives in Ogdensburgh, but owns house she rents in Wilmington.	4
Child, Mrs. Laura B.	24 Apr 1879	Died of paralysis 12 Apr 1879 at the residence of her son, Dr. N.N. Child in Ogdensburg. Former resident of Wilmington, and member of M.E. Church.	9
Child, Dr. N.N.	Death, n.d.	His mother, Mrs. Laura B. Child, aged 70, died 12 Apr 1879 in Wilmington.	8

Alphabetical Order by Person listed			
Name Mentioned	Date	Subject	Scrapbook Page
Child, Dr. N.N.	24 Apr 1879	From Ogdensburg. Son of Mrs. Laura B. Child, who died at his home 12 Apr 1879.	9
Clark, Mr.	13 Jan 1881	"Are spending a few days in Clintonville."	18
Clark, Charley	16 Apr 1881	He and wife gave great sugar party.	19
Clark, Charley	21 Apr 1881	Hosted a sugar party Apr 15.	20
Clark, Mrs. Charley	14 Jul 1880	From Clintonville. Is visiting her father, Abner Hickok.	16
Clark, Mrs. Charley	21 Apr 1881	Quite sick.	20
Clark, Mrs. Charley	5 May 1881	"May be improving."	20
Clemons, Noble	Marriage, n.d.	From Essex. Grandfather of Miss Nellie Shumway, who married Vivion W. Ruffner, both of Chicago.	9
Colby, George	21 May [1878]	Dangerously ill with typhoid and lung fever. At home of his employer, S.G. Williams.	5
Colby, George	13 Jun [1878]	Still dangerously ill.	5
Colby, George	16 Apr [1879]	Sentenced to 10 days in jail for stealing a hat.	9
Cole, _____	21 Apr 1880	Joseph Miles "has taken the Cole farm."	15
Cole, Mr.	30 Jul 1879	From Black Brook. Repairing his house in Wilmington.	11

Alphabetical Order by Person listed			
Name Mentioned	Date	Subject	Scrapbook Page
Cole, Mr. and Mrs. George	Birth n.d.	A son born to 9 Dec 1877 in North Stockholm.	2
Comstock, Allen	13 Aug 1880	Died. A former resident of Wilmington.	16
Comstock, Peter	Marriage, n.d.	The "late." His granddaughter is Miss Minnie L. White who married at Middle Granville 10 Dec 1879 Edward W. Harringan of Comstocks. His son-in-law is Geo. C. White of Middle Granville (Minnie's father.)	11
Conaboy, Miss	15 May [1878]	Has 25 scholars in ABC class.	5
Conaboy, Miss	14 Aug 1878	Her school's "closing exercises" and Thank You gifts from students.	6
Conaboy, Bidney	5 Dec 1877	Will teach school at North Elba.	2
Conaboy, Bidney	22 Mar 1878	Acted in play at Wilmington M.E. Church.	4
Conaboy, Miss Bidney	25 Apr 1878	Will teach Wilmington's Summer school.	5
Conerboy, Bidney	Marriage n.d.	From Wilmington. Married Byron R. Brewster of North Elba 19 Mar 1879 at AuSable Forks American House.	8
Conger, Mr.	4 Jul [1878]	Takes in burned-out Alpheus Perry family.	6
Conger, Mr.	2 Oct 1879	Off to Willsborough, where his wife's father is " said to be dying."	12

Alphabetical Order by Person listed			
Name Mentioned	Date	Subject	Scrapbook Page
Conger, Mr.	19 May 1880	25 five-cord coal pits of his at Upper Forge burned. Coal was destined for W.F. Weston's forge.	15
Conger, Mrs.	25 Apr 1878	"Dangerously ill."	5
Conger, Mrs.	29 Aug 1878	May be fatally ill.	6
Conger, Mrs.	30 Jul 1879	Is ill.	11
Conger, J.W.	14 Jul 1880	On Wilmington's committee on building.	16
Conger, J.W.	2 Mar 1881	Hired to build a wooden bridge for $431. Cassius Winch off job.	18
Conger, Justice	16 Apr [1879]	Sentenced George Colby to 10 days in jail for stealing a hat.	9
Conger, W.H.	22 Oct 1879	Closing remarks at M.E. Sunday School concert.	13
Conger, Mrs. W.J.	1 Jul [1879]	"Is failing," no recovery expected.	10
Conger, Mr. and Mrs. W.J.	Birth, n.d.	Daughter born to 9 Jun 1879 in Wilmington.	8
Cooper, Minor	24 Nov [1880]	Selling Singer sewing machines.	[17]
Cooper, Minor	17 Jun [1881]	Broke his leg while wrestling.	20
Cooper, Mr. Minor	14 Oct [1880]	Lost a yoke of cattle.	[17]
Cooper, Plin	16 Apr [1879]	Has resided in the far West for 20 years, now home on a visit.	9
Cooper, Plin	30 Apr [1879]	A reunion of his relatives held at his mother's. He is visiting from "his far distant home." He grew up in Wilmington.	9

Alphabetical Order by Person listed

Name Mentioned	Date	Subject	Scrapbook Page
Corle, Lon	13 Dec 1877	Member of gang of thieves.	2
Corwin, Mr.	27 Feb 1880	From Wilmington. An adult who spoke at Wilmington village school graduation.	14
Cronan, Patsy	Marriages n.d.	Rev. Father Fitzgerald married in AuSable Forks 3 May 1881, he from Chateaugay and Miss Ella Davy of Wilmington.	19
Crowley, Thomas	Deaths, n.d.	His sister-in-law, Mrs. John Harding died 10 Jul 1881 at his residence in Wilmington.	20
Crowley, Mr. And Mrs. James	Births, n.d.	A son born to 8 Feb 1881 in AuSable Forks.	18
Crowly, Mr.	2 Mar 1881	Recommends his election.	18
Crowly, Thomas	4 Apr 1878	Bought A. Fletcher's farm.	4
Davies, Brother	20 Nov [1877]	Preached at "conference" in Wilmington.	1
Davies, Brother	5 Dec 1877	Leads revival in Jay.	2
Davies, Mr.	22 Oct 1877	Pastor M.E. Church, Wilmington.	1
Davies, Mr. and Mrs.	1 Mar 1878	Attended Weston social.	4
Davies, Rev. R.J.	13 Dec 1877	"Our beloved pastor" receives a gift from his "friends."	2
Davies, Rev. R.J.	20 Apr 1878	"Has gone to conference."	4
Davies, Rev. R.J.	21 May [1878]	Wilmington M.E. Church Sabbath School under his supervision.	5

Alphabetical Order by Person listed			
Name Mentioned	Date	Subject	Scrapbook Page
Davies, Rev. R.J.	23 Feb [1879]	Began a series of religious meetings. Will leave in Spring.	8
Davies, Rev. R.J.	24 Apr 1879	Delivered his final sermon. At Wilmington and Jay for three years.	9
Davies, Rev. R.J.	13 Feb [1880]	Now at Luzerne; "our former pastor."	14
D'Avignon, Dr.	28 Apr [1880]	Called to consult with Dr. Wm. S.P. Fuller.	15
D'Avignon, Dr.	21 Apr 1881	Caring for Mrs. Ira Storrs.	20
D'Avignon, Dr.	10 Jul 1879	Dr. attending to Charlie Fish.	11
Davy, Mr.	4 Jul [1878]	Gathering clothes, etc. for burned-out-Alpheus Perry family.	6
Davy, Miss Ella	Marriage n.d.	Rev. Father Fitzgerald married in AuSable Forks 3 May 1881 she from Wilmington and Patsy Cronan of Chateaugay.	19
Davy, Miss Ella	5 May 1880	Will teach at Markhamville.	15
Davy, Miss Ella	15 Sept 1880	Very ill.	[17]
Davy, Lissie	9 Mar 1881	Recited at Wilmington village school closing exercises.	19
Davy, Lizzy	21 Jul [1881]	Recites at village school closing ceremonies.	21
Davy, Michael	14 Jul 1880	"Is carrying on Charles Fyans farm."	16
Day, Charley	6 Aug [1879]	From Plattsburg. Together with Mr. and Mrs. Isham and F.M. Hickok, visited L. Bliss.	11

Alphabetical Order by Person listed			
Name Mentioned	Date	Subject	Scrapbook Page
Day, Charley	26 Aug 1879	From Plattsburgh will deliver, set up, and demonstrate M.E. Church's new organ.	12
Day, Charley	11 Sept 1879	From Plattsburg. With Mr. McIntyre of AuSable Forks, delivered new organ to Wilmington's M.E. Church.	12
Dergin, Mrs. Ed	1 Jul [1879]	"Seriously ill with fits."	10
Dergin, Mr. and Mrs. E.	Births, n.d.	A son born to 18 Oct 1879 in Wilmington.	11
Dibble, Master Normy	1 Jul [1879]	From Keene. Visited us.	10
Dibble, William	1 Jul [1879]	From Keene. Visited us.	10
Dilno, Miss Sophrona	25 Sept 1879	"Quite sick with cholera."	12
Dirgin, Mrs. Ed.	5 May 1880	"Quite sick with measles."	15
Ditson, Oliver	20 Nov [1877]	Sermon published by.	1
Docum, Miss	21 Feb [1880]	In Wilmington. Selling "electric medals."	14
Edmonds, Lucy	13 Dec 1877	A madam (house of prostitution on Pebble St.), and co-leader of theft ring.	2
Estes, Lucena	31 Dec 1877	From Keene. Teaches school in "Elijah Weston's district."	3
Evans, George	15 Sept 1880	Dangerously ill.	[17]
Evans, Miss Lute	10 Jul [1878]	From Saranac Lake, visiting Mr. Amos and Sanford Avery's.	6

Alphabetical Order by Person listed			
Name Mentioned	Date	Subject	Scrapbook Page
Everett, Mr. F.E.	27 Feb 1880	From Malone. Selling organs in Wilmington.	14
Everett, Mr. F.E.	11 Apr 1880	Sets up John Hinds' new organ.	14
Everett, J.E.	7 Aug [1880]	Sold an organ to John Nye.	16
Farmer, Ann	13 Dec 1877	Prostitute in Madam Lucy Edmonds house.	2
Fay, Mr. A.	23 Dec 1877	"Lost" a cow.	3
Fay, John	22 Mar 1876	Acted in play at Wilmington M.E. Church.	4
Fay, Mrs. Nelson	17 Aug [1881]	Returned to Vermont, accompanied by her brother, Wallace	21
Featherston, Mr.	13 Nov [1880]	Pallbearer at funeral of Mrs. Kemp, mother of E.S. Kemp, at AuSable Forks Episcopal Church.	[17]
Featherston, Mr. E.	27 Jan 1881 (AuSable Forks)	Bought E.S. Kemp's trotter, Brown Bob, for $2,500.	18
Ferrington, Mr. and Mrs. George	22 Mar 1878	From Saranac; visiting friends in Wilmington.	4
Fish, Charlie	10 Jul 1879	Suffered an ugly wound to head while drunk on 4th.	11
Fish, Charlie	10 Jul 1879	Baby boy arrived at his house recently.	11
Fish, Charlie	17 July 1879	Has recovered from his injuries.	11
Fish, Charlie	4 Aug 1881	Makes and repairs carriages. Shop at South end of bridge.	21
Fish, Chas.	30 Jul 1879	Complainant in assault and battery case being tried at North Elba.	11

Alphabetical Order by Person listed			
Name Mentioned	Date	Subject	Scrapbook Page
Fish, Chas.	13 Aug [1879]	Fined $10 for assault on S.G. Williams in assault and battery case tried at North Elba.	11
FitzGerald, Mr.	Obit, n.d.	From Black Brook. Conducted funeral of Susan E. McLeod Washburn, who died 10 Aug 1879.	10
Fitzgerald, Rev. Father	Marriages n.d.	Married in AuSable Forks 3 May 1881 Patsy Cronan of Chateaugay and Miss Ella Davy of Wilmington.	19
Fletcher, Mrs.	9 Mar 1881	From North Elba. Guest at Mr. Loami Bliss.	19
Fletcher, Mr. A.	22 Mar 1878	Quite ill.	4
Fletcher, Mr. A.	25 Mar 1878	Previously ill, now doing better.	4
Fletcher, Mr. A.	3 Apr 1878	Sold his farm to Thomas Crowly, and moved to North Elba.	4
Fletcher, Alexander	15 May 1878	Died about two weeks ago in North Elba.	5
Fletcher, Leander	22 Sept 1880	Has married.	[17]
Foote, Mr.	16 Jun 1880	An evangelist, spoke at Wilmington's M.E. Church.	16
Forbes, John	16 Apr 1881	Recovering.	19
Forbs, Mr.	n.d. (between 9 Mar and 6 Apr 1881)	Fell from bridge under repair. Quite ill.	19

Alphabetical Order by Person listed			
Name Mentioned	Date	Subject	Scrapbook Page
Forbs, John	6 Apr 1881	May die at any moment. Long time resident; currently Postmaster and Notary Public. Has held many positions in town.	19
Forbs, Justice	19 Dec 1877	Justice of the Peace.	2
Foster, Sylvester	13 Dec 1877	Member of gang of thieves. Escaped.	2
Foster, "Young"	19 Dec 1877	Arrested and convicted of crime.	2
Fox, Mrs. E.	4 Sept 1879	From Brooklyn, NY. Together with Mr. and Mrs. Charley Thompson of Winooski Falls, VT, and Mrs. E.S. Kemp of AuSable Forks were guests of J. Hinds.	12
Frary, Hon. Asa	14 Oct [1880]	From Sutton, P.Q. He and daughter visiting John Hinds.	[17]
French, Emma	27 Feb 1880	Presented "Home Composition" at Wilmington's village school's graduation exercises.	14
French, Emma	9 Mar 1881	Recited at Wilmington village school closing exercises.	19
Fuller, ___	10 Jul 1879	Attending to Charlie Fish.	11
Fuller, Dr.	21 Apr 1881	Caring for Mrs. Ira Storrs.	20
Fuller, Dr.	5 May 1881	Attending to Mrs. Charley Clark.	20
Fuller, Mrs.	12 Mar 1879	From Mechum Lake. Daughter of Jasper Bliss. In town visiting friends.	8

Alphabetical Order by Person listed			
Name Mentioned	Date	Subject	Scrapbook Page
Fuller, Mr. and Mrs. A.	25 Mar 1878	From Mechum Lake. In town visiting friends.	4
Fuller, Mrs. Lou	9 Mar 1881	She, and son, from Mechum Lake expected in town	19
Fuller, Dr. Wm. S.P.	28 Apr [1880]	Called Dr. D'Avignon to consult on difficult case.	15
Fuller, Dr. Wm. St. P.	6 Apr 1881	Attending to terminally ill John Forbes.	19
Fyan, Charles	26 May 1880	Badly hurt his hand at Arnold Hill mine. Now at home	15
Fyan, Charles	9 Mar 1881	Will be moving to Palmer Hill, and rent his farm to Frank Jourdan of Jay.	19
Fyan, Mr. And Mrs.	14 Oct [1880]	A son and daughter born to 8 Nov 1880 in Wilmington Charles	[17]
Fyans, Bid	14 Aug 1878	Makes "Thank You" present for teacher.	6
Fyans, C.	2 Jan [1879]	Is mining at Clayburg.	7
Fyans, C.	23 Jan [1879]	Victim of theft of oats and pork.	7
Fyans, Charles	13 Jun [1878]	Lost a sheep.	5
Fyans, Charles	19 Jun [1878]	Building new barn.	5
Fyans, Charles	27 Dec [1878]	Theft of his buckwheat.	7
Fyans, Charles	26 Mar 1879	Rented his farm to Frank Hatch.	9
Fyans, Mr. and Mrs. Charles	Births, n.d.	Twin daughters born to 24 Jan 1880 in Wilmington	13

Alphabetical Order by Person listed			
Name Mentioned	Date	Subject	Scrapbook Page
Gaines, Mrs.	9 Jun 1880	From Keeseville. She and her two sisters visiting her daughter, Mrs. D.B. Hays.	15
Gaines, Mr. And Mrs. Fred	22 Sept 1880	Their daughter an excellent speaker at Sunday School picnic.	[17]
Gaines, Mrs. (Eva) William	29 Aug 1878	Visiting from Virginia. Originally from Wilmington.	6
Gaines, Mrs. William	21 Jul [1881]	From Virginia. Visiting in town.	21
Galusha, Capt. A.L.	25 Jan 1880	"P.M. of East Franklin, VT." He and wife guests at John Hinds. Have visited friends in Chazy, Keeseville, Clintonville, and AuSable Forks.	13
Galusha, Mr. And Mrs. A.W.	15 May 1881	From Ogdensburg. Together with Mr. and Mrs. Kemp of AuSable Forks, are visiting.	20
Galusha, J.W.	12 Mar 1879	From North Lawrence. Subscribing to newspaper.	8
Galusha, Wesley	30 Apr [1879]	Died 21 Apr, aged 83, at home in Sutton Falls, P.Q. of his granddaughter, Mrs. William Sears.	9
Galusha, Wm.	15 May [1878]	Spent Winter with friends in Wilmington and now visiting in St. Armand.	5
Galusha, William	Obit, n.d.	Died in Ogdensburg 4 Aug 1878. Short biography of.	6

Alphabetical Order by Person listed			
Name Mentioned	Date	Subject	Scrapbook Page
Galusha, Elder William	13 Nov [1880]	His youngest daughter, Mrs. Kemp, died in AuSable Forks at home of her son E.S. Kemp.	[17]
Gaskell, Leroy	Marriage, n.d.	From Clintonville. On 1 Jan 1879 marries Miss Ida Owen of AuSable Chasm, in Peru, at M.E. Parsonage, by Rev. Lewis.	8
Gaskill, Leroy	12 Mar 1879	Visits from Clintonville.	8
Gaskill, Mr. and Mrs. Leroy	Births, n.d.	A daughter born to 20 Nov 1879 in Chesterfield.	11
Gaskill, Mr. and Mrs. Leroy	4 Nov [1880]	From Clintonville. "We enjoyed a pleasant call from." Evidently Mrs. is "Osceola."	[17]
Gaskill, Mr. and Mrs. Leroy	17 Aug [1881]	From Clintonville. Visiting in town. Will tour lakes	21
Gattle, Mr.	5 May 1880	In town, "the new styles [will] flourish now."	15
Gattles	21 May 1878	Evidently makes and/or sells ladies hats. An intinerant	10
George, Miss Bertha	15 May 1881	Together with Miss Gracie George, both of Keeseville, in town.	20
George, Miss Gracie	14 Jul 1880	From Keeseville. Visiting her grandfather, David Hatch.	16
George, Miss Gracie	15 May 1881	Together with Miss Bertha George, both of Keeseville, in town.	20

Alphabetical Order by Person listed			
Name Mentioned	Date	Subject	Scrapbook Page
George, Hattie	23 Jan 1878	From Upper Jay. Attends church service in Wilmington	3
George, Oswin	22 Mar 1878	Acted in play at Wilmington M.E. church.	4
George, Samuel	Death, n.d.	Aged 69, died of consumption 26 Mar 1879 in Wilmington. An "old resident of Wilmington."	8
German, Thomas	13 Jun [1878]	Repairing house.	5
Goodrich, Mr.	19 Jun [1878]	An "experienced miller from Plattsburg," he bought James Bliss' gristmill property and intends to sell flour at low price.	5
Goodrich, Mr.	4 Jul [1878]	"Has concluded not to keep the Bliss mill property."	6
Gorman, Mr.	22 Oct 1877	Head (?) of "Select school."	1
Gorman, Mr.	12 Nov 1877	Rented his AuSable Forks hotel to Mr. Reed of Peru.	1
Gorman, Miss Bid	9 May 1879	Will teach at Franklin Falls.	9
Gorman, Bridget	12 Nov 1877	Teaching in Black Brook.	1
Gorman, Bridget	22 Mar 1878	Acted in play at Wilmington M.E. Church.	4
Gorman, Cornelius	9 Mar 1881	Recited at Wilmington village school closing exercises.	19

Alphabetical Order by Person listed			
Name Mentioned	Date	Subject	Scrapbook Page
Gorman, D.	30 Apr [1879]	Teacher at Wilmington village school.	9
Gorman, Dennis	20 Nov [1877]	Now teaching.	1
Gorman, Dennis	22 Mar 1878	Acted in play at Wilmington M.E. Church.	4
Gorman, Dennis	22 Mar 1878	Directed play at Wilmington M.E. Church.	4
Gorman, Dennis	25 Apr 1878	Attends school in Elizabethtown.	5
Gorman, Dennis	29 Aug 1878	To soon open a "select school" in village.	6
Gorman, Dennis	13 Sept 1878	Addressed Markhamville Sabbath School.	7
Gorman, Dennis	6 Mar [1879]	His school in village of Wilmington closed "with an exhibition of talent."	8
Gorman, Dennis	18 Mar [1879]	Selected to teach Wilmington village school during Summer.	8
Gorman, Dennis	27 Feb 1880	He and horse went through ice on pond. Both ok.	14
Gorman, Dennis	5 May 1880	Delivering nursery stock.	15
Gorman, Dennis	27 Jan 1881	Home from Malone.	18
Gorman, Miss Emma	27 Feb 1880	Visiting at Franklin Falls.	14
Gorman, Miss Emma	22 Sept 1880	Left to attend high school for two years.	[17]
Gorman, Miss Emma	15 May 1881	Has returned home.	20
Gorman, Maggie	12 Nov 1877	Teaching in Black Brook.	1

Alphabetical Order by Person listed			
Name Mentioned	Date	Subject	Scrapbook Page
Gorman, Maggie	22 Mar 1878	Acted in play at Wilmington M.E. Church.	4
Gorman, Miss Maggie	20 Apr 1878	Ill, but recovering.	4
[Gorman], Miss Maggie	9 May 1879	Will teach in the Potter district.	9
Gorman, Miss Maggie	22 Oct 1879	Recited at M.E. Sunday school concert.	13
Gorman, Miss Mary	16 Dec 1878	Will leave for Port Henry; teacher at graded school.	7
Gorman, Miss Mary	23 Dec 1880	Home from Port Henry.	[17]
Gorman, Miss Mary	27 Jan 1881	Returned to her school in Mineville.	18
Gorman, Miss Mary	22 Jun [1881]	Received a specimen box of Colorado minerals, as did Miss Effie Bliss, from the brothers Thomas Jr. and Mike Gorman of Colorado.	20
Gorman, Miss Mary	4 Aug 1881	"Teaching a select school here this fall."	21
Gorman, Mary A.	22 Mar 1876	Acted in play at Wilmington M.E. Church.	4
Gorman, Miss May	9 May 1879	Expected home from her school in Port Henry.	9
Gorman, Mike	22 Jun [1881]	Together with his brother, Thomas Jr. Gorman, both in Colorado, sent a specimen box of Colorado minerals to Miss Mary Gorman and Miss Effie Bliss.	20

Alphabetical Order by Person listed			
Name Mentioned	Date	Subject	Scrapbook Page
Gorman, Mr. T. Jr.	22 Mar 1878	Played music at Wilmington M.E. Church.	4
Gorman, Thomas	25 Apr 1878	Has bought the Patridge farm, that Mr. Lawrence recently bought.	5
Gorman, Thomas	29 Aug 1878	Painting his house.	6
Gorman, Thomas	16 Dec 1878	Finished his house remodeling.	7
Gorman, Thomas	23 Feb [1879]	Owns Clinton House in AuSable Forks.	8
Gorman, Thomas	26 Mar 1879	Purchase 12 acres from Monroe Hall. Land is near village and adjoins his farm.	9
Gorman, Thomas	23 Dec 1880	"Quite sick."	[17]
Gorman, Thomas`	27 Jan 1881	Mr. And Mrs. Nelly Hays are staying with.	18
Gorman, Thomas	21 Apr 1881	Quite ill, and being treated at the Adirondack House, AuSable Forks.	20
Gorman, Thomas Jr.	22 Mar 1878	Acted in play at Wilmington M.E. Church.	4
Gorman, Thomas Jr.	20 Apr 1878	On protracted visit to friends in Canada.	4
Gorman, Thomas Jr.	1 Apr [1879]	Left for Colorado to take up new occupation.	9
Gorman, Thomas Jr.	30 Apr [1879]	Writes home from Colorado.	9

Alphabetical Order by Person listed			
Name Mentioned	Date	Subject	Scrapbook Page
Gorman, Thomas Jr.	22 Jun [1881]	Together with his brother Mike Gorman, both in Colorado, sent a specimen box of Colorado minerals to Miss Mary Gorman, and Miss Effie Bliss.	20
Griffin, Elder	30 Jul 1879	Delivered sermon at Wilmington M.E. Church.	11
Hall, Mr.	16 Dec 1878	Owns saw mill; damaged in freshet.	7
Hall, Monroe	10 Jul [1878]	Store robbed.	6
Hall, Monroe	26 Mar 1879	Sold land near village to Thomas Gorman.	9
Haly, Edward	15 May 1878	Sold farm to Henry Hickok.	5
Hammond, Mr.	26 Mar 1879	Will manage W.F. Weston's farm during coming year.	9
Hammond, Mrs. C.	22 Oct 1879	Quite sick.	13
Hammond, Mr. and Mrs. Charles	Births, n.d.	A son born to 16 Apr 1881 in Wilmington.	19
Hamner, Thomas	2 Jan [1879]	Has moved to Jay.	7
Hanmer, Mr. and Mrs. Thomas	26 Aug 1879	From Redford. Visit Wilmington.	12
Harding, John	26 Jun 1878	Indicted by grand jury for "committing a base outrage upon a little girl"; has sold out and "left for parts unknown."	6
Harding, Mrs. John	Deaths, n.d.	Died in Wilmington 10 Jul 1881 at the residence of her brother-in-law, Thomas Crowley.	20

Alphabetical Order by Person listed			
Name Mentioned	Date	Subject	Scrapbook Page
Harding, Mrs. John	12 Jul 1881	Buried today in AuSable Forks.	20
Hardy, Mr. and Mrs.	20 Nov [1877]	Have adopted a "little orphan girl."	1
Hardy, A.	9 Oct 1879	Spoke at M.E. Church Sunday School picnic.	12
Hardy, Mrs. A.	17 Jun [1881]	Doing good job as Superintendant of Sabbath School.	20
Hardy, Amos	22 Oct 1877	Sabbath School recital.	1
Hardy, Amos	6 Aug [1879]	Donates $25 for purchase of organ for Wilmington M.E. Church.	11
Hardy, Amos	7 Aug [1880]	Miss Babbitt of Keeseville is visiting.	16
Hardy, Mrs. Amos	15 May 1881	Superintendant of M.E. Church Sabbath School.	20
Hardy, Mrs. Amos	17 Jun [1881]	Her mother, Mrs. Jones of Burlington, is visiting.	20
Hardy, George	21 May [1878]	Chosen librarian of Wilmington M.E. Sabbath School.	5
Hardy, Mr. and Mrs. George	Births, n.d.	In Wilmington, a son born to 17 Mar 1879.	8
Hardy, Miss L.	28 Apr [1880]	"Gave a quilting last week." This is "suspicious."	15
Hardy, Miss Lou	2 Mar 1881	Appointed to the Committee on Missions.	18
Hardy, Miss Lou	5 May 1881	Teaching school in Malbone district.	20
Hardy, Louis	22 Mar 1876	Acted in play at Wilmington M.E. Church.	4

Alphabetical Order by Person listed			
Name Mentioned	Date	Subject	Scrapbook Page
Hardy, Miss Lu	24 Jun [1880]	Visiting friends in Burlington and Vergennes.	16
Hardy, Miss Lu	14 Aug [1881]	Her school open. The children presented "her with enough pieced blocks for a nice bed quilt."	21
Hargraves, Mr.	13 Nov [1880]	Pallbearer at funeral of Mrs. Kemp, mother of E.S. Kemp, at AuSable Forks Episcopal Church.	[17]
Harmon, Rev.	21 Apr 1881	From Jay. Officiated, together with Rev. T. Watson, at Mrs. Frank Jordan's funeral at Wilmington Congregational Church, 9 Apr 1881.	20
Harper, Mrs. Wm.	19 Jun [1878]	From Keeseville, accompanied Mrs. David Hays from Massachusetts on visit to Hays' sister.	5
Harringan, Edward W.	Marriages n.d.	From Comstocks. Married at Middle Granville 10 Dec 1879 Miss Minnie L. White, daughter of Geo. C. White of Middle Granville, and granddaughter of the late Peter Comstock of Port Kent.	11
Harris, Smith	6 Apr 1881	Sold farm to William Wardner.	19
Hart, Mrs.	16 Apr [1879]	From Keeseville. To remove Jasper Bliss' facial cancers.	9

Alphabetical Order by Person listed

Name Mentioned	Date	Subject	Scrapbook Page
Hascall, Col. H.A..	6 Aug [1879]	U.S. Army. With H.S. Parkhurst of Gloversville, and their wives, are guests of Hon. W.F. Weston.	11
Haselton, Miss Rose		From Wilmington. Married Onias Wilkins in Wilmington by Rev. Thomas Watson at Congregational Parsonage 6 Dec 1879	11
Hatch, Father	22 Oct 1879	Gave M.E. Church Sunday School concert opening prayer.	13
Hatch, Anna	22 Oct 1879	Recited at M.E. Sunday School concert.	13
Hatch, Anna	27 Feb 1880	Presented essay at Wilmington's village school's graduation exercises.	14
Hatch, David	21 May [1878]	Lost a valuable cow.	5
Hatch, David	4 Sept 1879	Visited by Mr. and Mrs. Hoag of Keeseville.	12
Hatch, David	9 Oct 1879	Spoke at M.E. Church Sunday School picnic.	12
Hatch, David	21 Apr 1880	"Quite sick."	15
Hatch, David	28 Apr [1880]	"Still quite low."	15
Hatch, David	14 Jul 1880	His granddaughter, Miss Gracie George, from Keeseville, is visiting him.	16
Hatch, Frank	4 Jul [1878]	Donates clothes to burned-out Alpheus Perry family.	6
Hatch, Frank	26 Mar 1879	Is renting Charles Fyans' farm.	9

Alphabetical Order by Person listed			
Name Mentioned	Date	Subject	Scrapbook Page
Hatch, John	21 Jul [1881]	Recites at village school closing ceremonies.	21
Hathaway, Mr.	4 Jul [1878]	Manages Alpheus Perry's farm.	6
Hayes, Aaron	20 Nov [1877]	Victim of theft.	1
Hayes, Charley	22 Mar 1878	Acted in play at Wilmington M.E. Church.	4
Hayes, D.B.	15 Jan [1879]	Someone broke one of his house's windows.	7
Hayes, D.B.	14 Jul 1880	On Wilmington's committee on building.	16
Hayes, David	14 Aug 1878	On behalf of class presents "Thank You" gifts to teacher.	6
Hayes, David	24 Nov [1880]	Congregational Church Sabbath School Superintendent. At close of SS "received blocks enough for a large quilt from his scholars."	[17]
Hayes, Edwin	20 Nov [1877]	Victim of theft.	1
Hayes, Edwin	20 Apr 1878	"Has moved into the south wing of his father's house."	4
Hayes, Mr. and Mrs. Edwin	Births, n.d.	A daughter born to 22 Apr 1878 in Wilmington.	4
Hayes, Electa	22 Mar 1878	Acted in play at Wilmington M.E. Church.	4
Hayes, Mr. and Mrs. Elsworth	25 Mar 1878	Live in North Elba. Their "little son" died.	4

Alphabetical Order by Person listed			
Name Mentioned	Date	Subject	Scrapbook Page
Hayes, I.B.	30 Jul 1879	In Wilmington "canvassing for a new paper, called The Mountain Echo, to be published at AuSable Forks."	11
Hayes, Mattie	9 Mar 1881	Recited at Wilmington school closing exercises.	19
Hays, A.	9 Oct 1879	Spoke at M.E. Church Sunday School picnic.	12
Hays, Aaron	6 Nov 1877	Construction, improvements on farm.	1
Hays, Aaron	16 Dec 1878	"Newly clapboarded his house."	7
Hays, Aaron	1 Apr [1879]	His daughters sang at Jennie E. Mace's burial.	9
Hays, Aaron	25 Jun 1879	Runaway horse of Rollin Marshall in Markamville demolished his buggy.	10
Hays, Aaron	14 Feb [1880]	A cow of his broke her leg.	14
Hays, Aaron	9 Jun 1880	Has as guests, Edwin Hays and family of Stowers' Forge, and Charles Severance of Lewis.	15
Hays, Aaron	16 Jun 1880	Horse injured.	16
Hays, Charley	21 May [1878]	Together with Millard Hays has a camp at Conry Pond.	5
Hays, Charley	15 Sept 1880	Quite sick.	[17]
Hays, Charley	22 Sept 1880	Much better.	[17]

Alphabetical Order by Person listed			
Name Mentioned	Date	Subject	Scrapbook Page
Hays, Mrs. D.B.	9 Jun 1880	Visited by Mrs. Gaines of Keeseville, her mother, and mother's two sisters.	15
Hays, D.H.	15 Sept 1880	From AuSable Forks. His niece Miss Electa Hays is visiting.	[17]
Hays, Mrs. D.L.	22 Sept 1880	From AuSable Forks. In town last week.	[17]
Hays, David	16 Dec 1878	Sold village house to W.F. Weston and bought Millard Hays' place.	7
Hays, David	9 May 1879	Nearly completed his new house.	9
Hays, David	21 May 1879	"Has moved from the village into his new house on Pleasant street."	10
Hays, David	26 May 1880	Painting his house.	15
Hays, David	16 Jun 1880	Superintendant of Congregational Church.	16
Hays, David	15 May 1881	Elected Superintendent of Congregational Church Sabbath School.	20
Hays, Mrs. David	19 Jun [1878]	Her sister from Massachusetts visited, accompanied by Mrs. Wm. Harper of Keeseville.	5
Hays, Mr. and Mrs. David	10 Dec 1879	Celebrated their wedding anniversary with party.	13
Hays, Mr. and Mrs. David	22 Sept 1880	Enjoying guests from Keeseville and the West.	[17]
Hays, Edwin	21 May [1878]	Is employed by Miss Newman of North Elba and will soon move his family there.	5

Alphabetical Order by Person listed			
Name Mentioned	Date	Subject	Scrapbook Page
Hays, Edwin	2 Jan [1879]	Has moved into house previously occupied by Thomas Hamner.	7
Hays, Edwin	5 Jun 1879	He, and Cassius Winch, caught 60 lb of trout in 3 days "up the river."	10
Hays, Edwin	25 Jan 1880	Has moved to Lewis.	13
Hays, Edwin	9 Jun 1880	Edwin and family, of Stowers' Forge, together with Charles Severance of Lewis, visiting Aaron Hays.	15
Hays, Edwin	27 Jan 1881	Hurt himself.	18
Hays, Mrs. Edwin	14 Aug [1881]	"Very sick."	21
Hays, Miss Electa	21 May [1878]	Teaching school at Rodgers' kilns on the mountain road.	5
Hays, Miss Electa	22 Oct 1879	Recited at M.E. Sunday School concert.	13
Hays, Miss Electa	26 Nov 1879	Teaching in the Cooper district.	13
Hays, Miss Electa	30 Mar 1880	Will teach at the "upper forge."	14
Hays, Miss Electa	28 Apr [1880]	"Buying new furniture." This is "suspicious."	15
Hays, Miss Electa	15 Sept 1880	Visiting her Uncle D.H. Hays of AuSable Forks.	[17]
Hays, Miss Electa	2 Mar 1881	Appointed to the Committee on Missions.	18
Hays, Miss Electa	6 Apr 1881	Will teach at North Elba.	19
Hays, Elsworth	15 Jan 1878	A young (unnamed) hunter has arrived at his residence in North Elba.	3

Alphabetical Order by Person listed			
Name Mentioned	Date	Subject	Scrapbook Page
Hays, Mrs. Elsworth	1 Mar 1878	Visiting friends in Wilmington and Black Brook.	4
Hays, Gracie	21 Jul [1881]	Recites at village school closing ceremonies.	21
Hays, Jessie	21 Jul [1881]	Recites at village school closing ceremonies.	21
Hays, Miss Kit	6 Aug [1879]	Working at Stevens House in North Elba.	11
Hays, Kittie	27 Feb 1880	Read essay at Wilmington's village school's graduation exercises.	14
Hays, Kittie	9 Mar 1881	Elected to committee to get Dialogue Books of group to raise funds via exhibition for a church organ stool and chandeliers.	19
Hays, Miss Kittie	22 Oct 1879	Recited at M.E. Sunday School concert.	13
Hays, Miss Kittie	21 Apr 1880	"Has taken a school at Lewis."	15
Hays, Miss Kittie	28 Apr [1880]	"Commences her first school in Lewis, May 10th."	15
Hays, Miss Kittie	24 Nov [1880]	Teaching in the Weston District.	[17]
Hays, Miss Kittie	2 Mar 1881	Her school in Weston District will close.	18
Hays, Miss Kittie	15 May 1881	Teaching in the Stickney district at Franklin Falls.	20
Hays, Leonard	9 Mar 1881	From AuSable Forks. Visiting.	19
Hays, Miss Lillie	30 Apr [1879]	Teaches at Black Brook. Saw a catamount.	9

Alphabetical Order by Person listed			
Name Mentioned	Date	Subject	Scrapbook Page
Hays, Lucy	29 Aug 1878	Wife of James McDonald died. Service at M.E. Church.	6
Hays, Mattie	22 Oct 1879	Recited at M.E. Sunday School concert.	13
Hays, Mattie	27 Feb 1880	Spoke at Wilmington's village school's graduation exercises.	14
Hays, Mattie	21 Jul [1881]	Recites at village school closing ceremonies.	21
Hays, Millard	20 Nov [1877]	New house nearly complete. Will marry?	1
Hays, Millard	21 [May] 1878	Together with Charley Hays has a camp at Conry Pond.	5
Hays, Millard	16 Dec 1878	Sold his place to David Hays.	7
Hays, Mr. and Mrs. Nelly	27 Jan 1881	Are at Thomas Gorman's.	18
Hays, Mr. and Mrs. Nelly	2 Mar 1881	Have gone to Woods Falls.	18
Hays, Phebe	6 Aug [1879]	Working at Stevens House in North Elba.	11
Hays, Phebe	9 Mar 1881	Recited at Wilmington school exercises.	19
Hays, Phebe	17 Aug [1881]	Wed Alfred Wardner.	21
Hays, Miss Phebe	22 Oct 1879	Recited and sang at M.E. Sunday School concert.	13
Hays, Miss Phebe	27 Feb 1880	Presented essay at Wilmington's village school's graduation exercises.	14
Hays, Miss Phebe	n.d. [between 9Mar and 6 Apr 1881]	She will teach at school on the mountain.	19
Hazelton, Mr.	20 Apr 1878	Measles has struck this Mackhamville family.	4

Alphabetical Order by Person listed			
Name Mentioned	Date	Subject	Scrapbook Page
Hazelton, Daniel	12 Jun 1879	"The Commission in the lower part of town" improved road in Markhamville.	10
Hazelton, Daviel	30 Jul 1879	Has purchased a Meadow King Mower from J. Washer.	11
Henry, Charles	1 Mar 1878	A "young hunter."	4
Herald, J.T.	26 Nov 1879	A Commissioner. In town.	13
Hewitt, Miss	23 Jan 1878	From Upper Jay. Attends church service in Wilmington.	3
Hewitt, Mrs.	25 Sept 1879	Doing well with her select school.	12
Hewitt, Mrs.	12 Nov 1879	Her select school is closing.	13
Hewitt, Miss Clara	21 Feb [1880]	From St. Armand. Visiting friends.	14
Hewitt, Mrs. George	26 Aug 1879	From St. Armand. Will commence a select school in Wilmington.	12
Hewitt, Master V. Gilbert	21 [May] 1878	From Vermontville; visiting friends.	5
Hewitt, Mrs. P.V.	16 Jun 1880	Seriously ill.	16
Hewitt, Mrs. P.V.	29? Aug 1880	From Vermontville. Died. Daughter of Leonard Owen, a former resident of Wilmington.	16
Hewitt, Mr. and Mrs. P.V.	22 Mar 1878	From Vermontville; visiting friends in Wilmington.	4
Hewitt, Varnum	14 Aug 1878	From St. Armand; death of his daughter.	6

Alphabetical Order by Person listed			
Name Mentioned	Date	Subject	Scrapbook Page
Hichkok, Mr. and Mrs. Alexander	11 Sept 1879	From Ohio. Visiting. Formerly (up to 15 years ago) residents of Wilmington, then went to far West where they were not lucky.	12
Hickok, Mr.	21 Feb [1880]	Teaching at Wilmington village school.	14
Hickok, Mr.	9 Mar 1881	His school in village closed with recitations.	19
Hickok, Abner	Deaths, n.d.	Died 21 Feb 1881 in Wilmington. An "esteemed citizen." "For many years [he] held office of Deacon in the Congregational Church." Funeral services 23 Feb at Congregational Church, Rev. E.J. McKernan officiating.	18
Hickok, Abner	22 Oct 1879	Slowly recovering.	13
Hickok, Abner	14 Jul 1880	His daughter, Mrs. Charlie Clark of Clintonville is visiting.	16
Hickok, Abner	13 Jan 1881	Dangerously ill.	18
Hickok, Abner	27 Jan 1881	"Is no better."	18
Hickok, Mr. Abner	11 Sept 1879	Is ill.	12
Hickok, Albert	16 Dec 1878	Has returned to Kansas.	7
Hickok, Anna	23 Dec 1877	Home from Plattsburgh school.	3
Hickok, Miss Anna	21 May [1878]	Attending school at Plattsburgh.	5
Hickok, Miss Anna	19 Jun [1878]	Her new piano arrived.	5

Alphabetical Order by Person listed			
Name Mentioned	Date	Subject	Scrapbook Page
Hickok, Miss Anna	6 Mar [1879]	Is in Nashua, NH.	8
Hickok, Miss Anna	17 Aug [1881]	"Has returned home."	21
Hickok, Miss Annie	13 Jun [1878]	Studying painting in Plattsburgh.	5
Hickok, F.M.	29 May 1879	Visiting friends. Trying to sell organs?	10
Hickok, F.M.	6 Aug [1879]	Together with Mr. and Mrs. Isham and Charley Day, all of Plattsburgh, visited L. Bliss.	11
Hickok, F.M.	22 Oct 1879	Sang and gave closing remarks at M.E. Sunday School concert.	13
Hickok, Miss Fannie	12 Jun 1879	Will spend Summer with her Aunt, Mrs. John Merrill, of Omro, WI.	10
Hickok, Miss Fannie	24 Jun [1880]	At Clintonville, in milliner business.	16
Hickok, G.T.	20 Apr 1878	Moved into house owned by Mrs. Laura B. Child of Ogdensburgh.	4
Hickok, G.T.	30 Jul 1879	Defendant, with S.G. Williams, in assault and battery case being tried at North Elba.	11
Hickok, G.T.	13 Aug [1879]	His trial at North Elba for assault and battery postponed.	11
Hickok, Mr. and Mrs. Gilbert	Birth, n.d.	A son born to 7 May 1878 in Wilmington.	4

Alphabetical Order by Person listed			
Name Mentioned	Date	Subject	Scrapbook Page
Hickok, Miss Hannah	Marriages, n.d.	Married Nelson Sheldon 12 Mar 1881 at Wilmington's Congregational Parsonage. Married by Rev. Thomas Watson. Both of Wilmington.	19
Hickok, Henry	15 May [1878]	Has purchased the Edward Haly farm.	5
Hickok, Henry	10 Jul 1879	His daughter was injured in fall from load of hay.	11
Hickok, Mr. and Mrs. Henry	Birth, n.d.	Daughter born to 31 Dec 1878 in Wilmington.	8
Hickok, Miss Lelia	22 Oct 1879	Recited at M.E. Sunday School concert.	13
Hickok, Lola	14 Aug 1878	Reads paper at school's closing exercises.	6
Hickok, Lou	27 Feb 1880	Spoke at Wilmington's village school's graduation exercises.	14
Hickok, Miss Lou	27 Feb 1880	Won a spelling prize at Wilmington village school.	14
Hickok, Lula	9 Mar 1881	Recited at Wilmington village school closing	19
Hickok, Lula	21 Jul [1881]	Recites at village school closing ceremonies.	21
Hickok, Miss Paulina	16 Apr 1881	Visiting friends in Clintonville.	19
Hickok, Miss Pauline	19 Jun [1878]	Spending Summer with her aunt in St. Lawrence Co.	5
Hickok, R.	26 Mar 1879	With [his] daughter, Mrs. Ada Reeves, is visiting Bloomingdale friends.	9

Alphabetical Order by Person listed			
Name Mentioned	Date	Subject	Scrapbook Page
Hickok, R.	21 May 1879	The Sabbath School Assistant Superintendent and Superintendent of Singing for M.E. Church.	10
Hickok, R.	9 Oct 1879	Spoke at M.E. Church Sunday School picnic.	12
Hickok, R.	22 Oct 1879	Conducted singing at M.E. Sunday School concert.	13
Hickok, R.	22 Oct 1879	His daughter, Mrs. N. Pillsbury of Ohio visiting.	13
Hickok, R.	25 Dec [1879]	Received a Xmas gift from his M.E. Church choir.	13
Hickok, Mr. R.	22 Oct 1877	M.E. Sabbath School Superintendent.	1
Hickok, Mr. R.	5 Dec 1877	Will soon teach at AuSable Forks. Methodist chorister.	2
Hickok, Mr. R.	31 Dec 1877	Is quite ill.	3
Hickok, Mr. R.	3 Apr 1878	Teaching at AuSable Forks, but school closed due to epidemic. Will return to Wilmington.	4
Hickok, Mr. R.	13 Jun [1878]	Has new fence.	5
Hickok, Mr. R.	13 Sept 1878	Addressed Markhamville Sabbath School.	7
Hickok, Mr. R.	16 Apr [1879]	Has closed his singing school.	9
Hickok, Mr. R.	6 Aug [1879]	"Zealous worker" for Wilmington M.E. Church's musical department.	11

Alphabetical Order by Person listed			
Name Mentioned	Date	Subject	Scrapbook Page
Hickok, Mr. R.	26 Nov 1879	"An old and experienced teacher." Will teach "our village school."	13
Hickok, Mr. R.	27 Feb 1880	Wilmington village school teacher.	14
Hickok, Mr. R.	15 May 1881	Assistant chorister at M.E. Church Sabbath School.	20
Hickok, Rodgers	21 May [1878]	Chosen Assistant Superintendent and Superintendent of Singing of Wilmington M.E.	5
Hickok, Rogers	9 Mar 1881	Church Sabbath School. Elected manager of group to raise funds via an exhibition for a church organ stool and chandeliers.	19
Hickok, Wyat	22 Oct 1879	Visiting friends.	13
Hinds, Miss E.D.	22 Oct 1879	Sang at M.E. Sunday School concert.	13
Hinds, Emma	22 Oct 1877	Sabbath School recital.	1
Hinds, Emma	9 Mar 1881	Elected Treasurer of group to raise funds via an exhibition for a church organ stool and chandeliers.	19
Hinds, Ernest	17 Jul 1879	From Chateaugay. Visiting his father.	11
Hinds, H.L.	2 Jan [1879]	At Silver Lake.	7
Hinds, Henry	5 Dec 1877	Theft of his property.	2
Hinds, Henry	23 Dec 1877	A daughter injured herself.	3

Alphabetical Order by Person listed			
Name Mentioned	Date	Subject	Scrapbook Page
Hinds, Henry	10 Dec 1879	Lost a valuable cow.	13
Hinds, Mrs. Henry	21 Feb [1880]	"Quite sick."	14
Hinds, Herbert E.	Marriage, n.d.	From Wilmington. Marries Miss Abba Taylor of North Elba 16 Oct 1879. Married in Wilmington by Rev. Thomas Watsen.	11
Hinds, Herbert E.	6 Mar [1879]	From Wilmington. "Spending the Winter at Keene Flats." Visiting "us."	8
Hinds, Master Herbert	1 Jul [1879]	From Keene. Visited us.	10
Hinds, Hiram	7 Aug [1880]	"In town."	16
Hinds, Horace	21 May [1878]	Chosen Assistant Librarian of Wilmington M.E. Church Sabbath School.	5
Hinds, Horace	26 Mar 1879	Sold his farm to R.C. Lawrence.	9
Hinds, Horace	16 Apr [1879]	His farm sold to John Nye, instead of R.C. Lawrence. Nye then sold to Mr. Maynard.	9
Hinds, Mrs. Horace	12 Nov 1877	Killed a deer.	1
Hinds, J.	13 Sept 1878	Harvesting crops.	7
Hinds, J.	23 Feb [1878]	Is visited by E.S. Kemp and W. Benway of Frelighsburg, P.Q.	8

Alphabetical Order by Person listed			
Name Mentioned	Date	Subject	Scrapbook Page
Hinds, J.	4 Sept 1879	Visited by Mr. and Mrs. Charley Thompson of Winooski Falls VT, Mrs. E. Fox of Brooklyn NY, and Mrs. E.S. Kemp of AuSable Forks.	12
Hinds, John	16 Apr [1879]	"Thinks his crow tax is amply paid, for he lost nine nice pigs."	9
Hinds, John	10 Jul 1879	Has an unusual apple tree.	11
Hinds, John	22 Oct 1879	Elected Trustee at annual school meeting for 3 year term.	13
Hinds, John	27 Feb 1880	Ordered a Smith American organ from F.E. Everett of Malone.	14
Hinds, John	11 Apr 1880	His new organ arrived.	14
Hinds, John	14 Jul 1880	Mrs. John Ames of Clintonville and Miss Gracie Barney of Burlington, VT are guests of John Hinds.	16
Hinds, John	13 Aug 1880	"On a visit to friends down the river."	16
Hinds, John	29? Aug 1880	Daniel Stickney of Jay, and Mrs. E. Jucket of Poultney, VT, are his guests.	16
Hinds, John	14 Oct [1880]	The Hon. Asa Frary and daughter of Sutton, P.Q. visiting.	[17]
Hinds, John	9 Mar 1881	Has a span of 3 year old colts for sale.	19
Hinds, John	21 Apr 1881	Mrs. E.S. Kemp is his guest.	20

Alphabetical Order by Person listed			
Name Mentioned	Date	Subject	Scrapbook Page
Hinds, John	4 Aug 1881	Wasps spooked his horses while haying.	21
Hinds, Mrs. John	5 Jun 1879	Visiting her sister, R.F. Kemp, at AuSable Forks.	10
Hinds, Mrs. John	16 Jun 1880	"Quite ill."	16
Hinds, John S.	Obit, n.d.	Died 7 Aug 1879 in Keene, aged 76 years. Funeral service 9 Aug at Wilmington's M.E. Church, Rev. C.A. Bradford presiding.	10
Hinds, Mrs. John S.	Obit, n.d.	Aged about 75, resident of Wilmington "for a number of years," but "of Keene," died. Service at Wilmington by Rev. Thomas Watson. She was member of M.E. Church.	
Hinds, Lillian	22 Oct 1879	Recited at M.E. Sunday School concert.	13
Hinds, Lillian	9 Mar 1881	Recited at Wilmington school exercises.	19
Hinds, Lillian	21 Jul [1881]	Recites (twice) at village school closing ceremonies. She spoke first.	21
Hinds, Lillie	27 Feb 1880	Spoke at Wilmington's village school's graduation exercises.	14
Hinds, Richard	21 Apr 1880	"Agent for the original galvanic battery, direct from the professor, who invented them."	15
Hoag, Mr. and Mrs.	29 Aug 1878	From Keeseville. Visiting town.	6

Alphabetical Order by Person listed

Name Mentioned	Date	Subject	Scrapbook Page
Hoag, Mr. and Mrs.	4 Sept 1879	From Keeseville. Visiting David Hatch's.	12
Howe, Dr.	27 Jan 1881	From Black Brook. Successful with Wilmington patients.	18
Howe, Dr.	n.d. (between 9 Mar and 6 Apr 1881)	From Black Brook. Very skillful.	19
Howe, Dr.	5 May 1881	Attending to Mrs. Charley Clark.	20
Hoxie, Mr.	16 Dec 1878	From Sandy Hill; will repair James Bliss' grist mill.	7
Huntington, Mr.	4 Jul [1878]	Gathers clothes, etc. for the burned-out Alpheus Perry family.	6
Huntington, A.	22 Oct 1879	Recited at M.E. Sunday School concert.	13
Huntington, Amos	27 Feb 1880	Spoke at Wilmington's village school's graduation exercises.	14
Huntington, Amos	19 May 1880	"Quite sick with measles."	15
Huntington, Amos	9 Mar 1881	Recited at Wilmington school exercises.	19
Huntington, Amos	21 Jul [1881]	Recites (twice) at village school closing exercises.	21
Huntington, Clara	27 Feb 1880	Spoke at Wilmington's village school's graduation	14
Huntington, Clara	21 Jul [1881]	Recites (twice) at village school closing ceremonies.	21
Huntington, Ella	22 Mar 1878	Acted in play at Wilmington M.E. Church.	4
Huntington, Grey	21 Jul [1881]	Recites at village school closing ceremonies.	21

Alphabetical Order by Person listed			
Name Mentioned	Date	Subject	Scrapbook Page
Huntington, Guy	9 Mar 1881	Recited at Wilmington village school closing exercises.	19
Huntington, H.J.	9 Mar 1879	Architect for David Hays' new house.	9
Huntington, H.J.	28 Apr [1880]	"Will build new house."	15
Huntington, H.J.	13 Aug 1880	His new house nearly finished.	16
Huntington, Mr. and Mrs. H.J.	16 Dec 1878	Tenth wedding anniversary party-celebration for couple. Married 2 Dec 1868. Detailed description. Mrs.' sister is Miss Low.	7
Huntington, Henry	20 Nov [1877]	Has a harness shop.	1
Huntington, Henry	11 Apr 1880	"At the Forks working on the Adirondack House."	14
Huntington, Henry	9 Jun 1880	Moved his old house, and building new one.	15
Ingless, Mrs. Edmond	Obit, n.d.	Aged 37 years, died of typhoid dysentery 7 Oct 1878 at St. Armond, C[anada] E[ast].	4
Isham, Mr. And Mrs.	6 Aug [1879]	From Plattsburgh. Together with Charley Day and F.M. Hickok, visited L. Bliss.	11
Jaques, Guy	Death, n.d.	Aged 5 years. Died of diphtheria 8 May 1879 in Wilmington. Youngest son of Mr. and Mrs. Timothy Jaques	8
Jaques, Mr. and Mrs.Timothy	Death, n.d.	Son, Guy, aged 5 died 8 May 1879 in Wilmington.	8

Alphabetical Order by Person listed			
Name Mentioned	Date	Subject	Scrapbook Page
Jaquis, Mr. Jas	30 Jul 1879	Received a pension of about $1300.	11
Jaquis, Timothy	14 Jul 1880	His daughter dislocated her shoulder while raspberrying.	16
Jaquis, Timothy	7 Jul 1881	Buying butter, eggs and poultry for hotels on Lake Placid.	20
Jaquish, Ed.	24 Nov [1880]	Last Sabbath in Keene accidentally shot himself. Buried 23rd in Wilmington. Leaves wife and 1 child.	[17]
Jaquish, Etta	9 Mar 1881	Recited at Wilmington village school closing exercises.	19
Jaquish, Phil	9 Mar 1881	Recited at Wilmington village school closing exercises.	19
Johnes, Miss	21 May [1878]	From North Jay and teaching school in E. Weston's district.	5
Jones, Mrs.	17 Jun [1881]	From Burlington. Visiting her daughter, Mrs. Amos Hardy.	20
Jones, Miss Nettie	14 Aug 1878	Teaches the school in E. Weston's district.	6
Jordan, Mrs. Frank	21 Apr 1881	Died. Buried 9 Apr 1881 in Wilmington. Daughter of Albert Wilkins of Wilmington. Married "scarcely a year." Funeral services at Congregational Church, Rev. Harmon of Jay, and Rev. T. Watson of Wilmington officiated.	20

Alphabetical Order by Person listed			
Name Mentioned	Date	Subject	Scrapbook Page
Jourdan, Frank	9 Mar 1881	From Jay. Will rent Charles Fyan's farm.	19
Jourdan, Frank	16 Apr 1881	His farm not "hired by Mr. R.C. Lawrance after all."	19
Jucket, Mrs. E.	29? Aug 1880	From Poultney, VT. She and Daniel Stickney of Jay are guests of John Hinds.	16
Keeves, Mrs. Ada	21 May 1879	The Librarian of M.E. Church Sabbath School.	10
Kemp, _____	16 Apr [1879]	He and Benway will take possession of Clinton House in AuSable Forks this month.	9
Kemp, Mrs.	13 Nov [1880]	She died at AuSable Forks. Is youngest daughter of Elder William Galusha, and born in St. Armand, P.Q. A member of Episcopal Church. Funeral held 9 Nov 1880 at Episcopal Church in AuSable Forks. Charles Kendal in charge of funeral. Pallbearers; Messrs Hargraves, Featherton, Pierce, and Petit. Rev. Charles Bragdon officiated.	[17]
Kemp, E.S.	23 Feb [1879]	From Frelightsburg, P.Q. visits J. Hinds. Is negotiating to lease Clinton House in AuSable Forks.	8
Kemp, E.S.	30 Apr [1879]	Arrived in Wilmington. Shortly will open his AuSable Forks hotel.	9

Alphabetical Order by Person listed			
Name Mentioned	Date	Subject	Scrapbook Page
Kemp, E.S.	21 May 1879;	Took possession of Adirondack House (formally called Clinton House) at AuSable Forks.	10
Kemp, E.S.	5 Jun 1879	Kemp formally of Frelighsburgh, P.Q.	
Kemp, E.S.	13 Nov [1880]	His mother, Mrs. Kemp, died at his house in AuSable Forks.	[17]
Kemp, E.S.	27 Jan 1881(AuSable Forks)	Sold his trotter, Brown Bob, to Mr. E. Featherston, for $2,500.	18
Kemp, Mr. E.S.	28 Jan 1881(AuSable Forks)	"Gone to Canada on business."	18
Kemp, Mrs. E.S.	30 Jul 1879	Together with Master Frankie, is visiting from AuSable Forks.	11
Kemp, Mrs. E.S.	4 Sept 1879	From AuSable Forks. Together with Mr. And Mrs. Charley Thompson of Winooski Falls VT, and Mrs. E. Fox of Brooklyn NY, were guests of J. Hinds.	12
Kemp, Mrs. E.S.	21 Apr 1881	A guest of John Hinds.	20
Kemp. Mr. and Mrs. E.S.	Births, n.d.	In AuSable Forks a son born 6 Mar 1880 to.	14
Kemp. Mr. and Mrs. E.S.	Deaths, n.d.	Their son, Roy, died in AuSable Forks 14 May 1880 of cholera. Funeral held on Sat.	15
Kemp. Mr. and Mrs. E.S.	1 Jul [1879]	"Called to-day," businesses good.	10
Kemp. Mr. and Mrs. E.S.	26 May 1880	Guest at J. Hinds'.	15

Alphabetical Order by Person listed			
Name Mentioned	Date	Subject	Scrapbook Page
Kemp. Mr. and Mrs. E.S.	15 May 1881	From AuSable Forks. Together with Mr. And Mrs. A.W. Galusha of Ogdensburg, are visiting friends.	20
Kemp, Master Frankie	30 Jul 1879	Together with Mrs. E.S. Kemp, is visiting from AuSable Forks.	11
Kemp, Mrs. K.F.	30 Jul 1879	Visited friends in town.	11
Kemp, R.F.	5 Jun 1879	Mrs. John Hinds' sister at AuSable Forks.	10
[Kemp], Roy	[Deaths], n.d.	Son of Mr. and Mrs. E.S. Kemp died in AuSable Forks 14 May 1880 of cholera.	15
Kemdal, Charles	13 Nov [1880]	In charge of funeral for Mrs. Kemp, mother of E.S. Kemp, at AuSable Forks Episcopal Church.	[17]
Kendall, Dr. Frank	18 Mar [1880]	From Jay. Attending 2 families in Wilmington.	14
Kennedy, Mr. M.	22 Mar 1878	Played music at Wilmington M.E. Church.	4
Kernan, Rev. E.J.	18 Mar [1880]	Continuing his "protracted effort," with much success, at M.E. Church.	14
Kilborn, Mrs. D.	25 Jun 1879	Neighbor's dog damages her house.	10
Kilborn, David	Obit, n.d.	Aged 60, died at Wilmington residence of Aaron Hayes on 14 Nov 1877.	1
Kilborn, David	6 Nov 1877	Partial paralysis.	1

Alphabetical Order by Person listed			
Name Mentioned	Date	Subject	Scrapbook Page
Kilborn, Norman	29 May 1879	Now a lawyer in Illinois. Originally from Wilmington. Will visit this Summer.	10
Kilborn, Norman	29? Aug 1880	From Illinois. "Home on a visit."	16
Kilborn, Norman	22 Sept 1880	Is returning to Illinois.	[17]
Kilborn, Norman	22 Sept 1880	From Illinois. Addressed Wilmington's Republican meeting.	[17]
Kilborn, Preston	27 Feb 1880	Spoke at Wilmington's village school's graduation exercises.	14
Kilborn, Preston	24 Nov [1880]	Badly cut his foot.	[17]
Kilburn, David	12 Nov 1877	Died at Aaron Hays residence.	1
Knapp, D.S.	21 May 1879; 5 Jun 1879	Printer misread Rupert's handwriting, D.S. Knapp of AuSable Forks and formally of Frelighsburgh, P.Q., is really E.S. Kemp.	10
Lamb, Fred	Marriage, n.d.	From North Elba. On 1 Jan 1878 marries Carrie A. Nash of North Elba at Wilmington's Congregational Parsonage by Rev. T. Watson.	8
Lamoy, Henry	15 Sept 1880	Moved into upper part of L. Bliss' house.	[17]
Lamoy, McDonald	Marriage, n.d.	Married Miss Addie Preston 29 Jun 1879 in Jay by Rev. E.J. McKernon. Both bride and groom reside in Wilmington.	5

Alphabetical Order by Person listed			
Name Mentioned	Date	Subject	Scrapbook Page
LaMoy, Mr. and Mrs. McDonald	5 May 1880	A son born to 1 May 1880 in Wilmington.	15
Lamoy, William	5 Dec 1877	He and his son sold their farm to Mr. Ashley Prime of Upper Jay.	2
Lansing, Miss Emma	11 Sept 1879	From Plattsburgh. Formerly of Wilmington. Visiting with Mrs. Wm. Spafford of Plattsburg.	12
Lansing, W.	26 Aug 1879	From Keeseville. Visits Wilmington.	12
Lawrence, Mr.	25 Apr 1878	Will live on farm he has rented to Mr. R. Marshall.	5
Lawrence, Asa	21 Jul [1881]	Recites at village school closing ceremonies.	21
Lawrence, R.C.	31 Dec 1877	Sold his farm to Rollin Marshall. Is excellent citizen.	3
Lawrence, R.C.	8 May 1878	Has purchased the Ned O'Neil and Hiram Patridge farms, the latter previously occupied by Joseph Miller.	5
Lawrence, R.C.	25 Apr 1878	School district Trustee. Has hired Bidney Conaboy.	5
Lawrence, R.C.	19 Jun [1878]	Building Charles Fyans new barn.	5
Lawrence, R.C.	23 Feb [1879]	Plans to repair his house in Spring.	8
Lawrence, R.C.	26 Mar 1879	Bought Horace Hinds' farm.	9
Lawrence, R.C.	16 Jun 1880	Bought Pay place, and let it to Peter Shumway.	16
Lawrence, R.C.	14 Jul 1880	On Wilmington's committee on building.	16

Alphabetical Order by Person listed

Name Mentioned	Date	Subject	Scrapbook Page
Lawrence, Mr. R.C.	16 Apr 1881	Has hired the Chas. Fyan farm, not the Frank Jourdan.	19
Lawrence, Zach	21 Apr 1880	Is running W.F. Watson's new kilns.	15
Lawrence, Zach	21 Apr 1880	Fred Winch has moved onto his farm.	15
Leavens, Linus	25 Aug 1879 East Franklin, VT	Obit for, d. 20 Aug 1879 at Berkshire Center VT.	0
Leavens, Miss Marietta	26 Aug 1879 East Franklin, VT	Daughter of Linus Leavens.	0
Leavens, Penuel	25 Aug 1879 East Franklin VT	Father of Linus Leavens.	0
Leavens, Sally (Cross)	25 Aug 1879 East Franklin VT	Mother of Linus Leavens.	0
Lewis, Mr.	26 Nov [1877]	Slowly improving.	2
Lewis, Mrs.	12 Mar 1879	Gone to North Elba to visit daughter, Mrs. Lyon.	18
Lewis, Addie L.	Marriage, n.d.	From Wilmington. On 31 Dec 1878 marries Ira B. Lyon of North Elba, at Wilmington's Congregational Parsonage by Rev. T. Watson.	
Lewis, Mrs. John	1 Nov [1877]	"Dangerously ill."	1
Lewis, Mr. and Mrs. John	Birth, n.d.	A son born to, in Wilmington, 1 Jun 1878.	5
Lewis, Rev.	Marriage, n.d.	Marries Leroy Gaskell and Ida Owen at M.E. Parsonage in Peru, 1 Jan 1879.	8
Ling, Mrs.	17 Aug [1881]	Received a pension of about $1,500.	21

Alphabetical Order by Person listed			
Name Mentioned	Date	Subject	Scrapbook Page
Liston, Dr.	1 Nov [1877]	Plattsburgh doctor.	1
Liston, Dr.	26 Nov [1877]	Physician.	2
Loammi, Mr.	6 Aug [1879]	Has a surplus of "sporting custom[ers]" and thus had "to send many applicants to the hotel."	11
Low, Miss	16 Dec 1878	Sister of Mrs. H.J. Huntington.	7
Lucas, Mr. and Mrs. A.G.	26 Aug 1879	From Burlington, VT. Visited Wilmington.	12
Lyon, Mrs.	12 Mar 1879	Daughter of Mrs. Lewis. Lives in North Elba.	8
Lyon, Ira B.	Marriage, n.d.	From North Elba. On 31 Dec 1878 marries Addie L. Lewis of Wilmington, at Wilmington's Congregational Parsonage by Rev. T. Watson.	8
Lyon, Mrs. Ira	21 Apr 1880	She and son in town.	15
Lyon, Mr. and Mrs. Ira B.	Births, n.d.	A son born to 18 Oct 1879 in North Elba.	11
McDonald, James	29 Aug 1878	His wife, Lucy Hays, died. Services at M.E. Church.	6
McIntyre, Mr.	11 Sept 1879	From AuSable Forks with Charley Day of Plattsburg delivered new organ to Wilmington's M.E. Church.	12
McKernan, Bro.	25 Jun 1879	Delivers address to Sabbath School teachers and children.	10

Alphabetical Order by Person listed			
Name Mentioned	Date	Subject	Scrapbook Page
McKernan, Bro.	24 Jun [1880]	The Rev. E.J. McKernan, pastor of M.E. Church.	16
McKernan, Rev.	21 May 1879	"Our new pastor."	10
McKernan, Rev.	30 Jul 1879	Preached at Markhamville.	11
McKernan, Rev. E.J.	25 Sept 1879	With Rev. C.A. Bradform officiated at quarterly meeting.	12
McKernan, Rev. E.J.	9 Oct 1879	Gave closing address at M.E. Church Sunday School picnic.	12
McKernan, Rev. E.J.	25 Dec [1879]	Receives a $20 Xmas gift from his M.E. congregation.	13
McKernan, Rev. E.J.	25 Jan 1880	Holding a series of meetings at M.E. Church.	13
McKernan, Rev. E.J.	13 Feb [1880]	Holding a series of meetings at M.E. Church.	14
McKernan, Rev. E.J.	30 Mar 1880	Preached last sermon of conference year.	14
McKernan, Rev. E.J.	16 Jun 1880	Went fishing at North Elba, but caught only bug bites.	16
McKernan, Rev. E.J.	22 Sept 1880	Delivered remarks at Sunday School picnic, as did Rev. Thomas Watson.	[17]
McKernan, Rev. E.J.	Deaths, n.d.	Officiated at funeral of Abner Hickok at Wilmington's Congregational Church 23 Feb 1881.	18
McKernan, Rev. E.J.	5 May 1881	"Our pastor for another year."	20

Alphabetical Order by Person listed			
Name Mentioned	Date	Subject	Scrapbook Page
McKernon, Rev. E.J.	Marriage, n.d.	Marries couple in Jay.	5
McLeod, Byron	17 Jul 1879	Assistant Superintendent of Markhamville Sabbath School.	11
McLeod, Mr. and Mrs. Enoch	Birth, n.d.	A son born to, 1 Mar 1879, in Wilmington.	18
McLeod, Jefferson	Obit, n.d.	Father of Susan E. McLeod Washburn, who died 10 Aug 1879.	10
McLeod, Miss Lottie	12 Nov [1879]	Will teach at Franklin Falls during Winter.	13
Mace, A.	6 Aug [1879]	From AuSable. With Dr. J. Sanford, visiting Rupert's family	11
Mace, Mr. Amasa	12 Jul 1881	From Millersville. In town selling pickerel.	20
Mace, Mr. and Mrs. Amasa	19 Apr 1881	From AuSable. With Miss Libbie Beardsley, visiting friends in town.	19
Mace, Jennie E.	Death, n.d.	Aged 2 years, 4 months. Died in AuSable 29 Mar 1878. Youngest child of Lester and Jennie Mace.	8
Mace, L.F.	15 May [1878]	His Vegetable Lung Remedy recommended. He lives in Keeseville NY.	5
Mace, L.F.	1 Apr [1879]	[Jennie E.], his daughter, [who died 29 Mar in AuSable], buried in Wilmington.	9
Mace, L.F.	28 Apr [1880]	Visiting.	15
Mace, Mrs. L.F.	26 Aug 1879	She and daughter visiting Wilmington friends.	12

Alphabetical Order by Person listed			
Name Mentioned	Date	Subject	Scrapbook Page
Mace, Mr. and Mrs. L.F.	15 May [1878]	Visited "us" last week.	5
Mace, Mr. and Mrs. L.F.	11 Apr 1880	From Clintonville. Visiting.	14
Mace, Lester and Jennie	Death, n.d.	Their youngest child, Jennie E., died in AuSable 29 Mar 1878. Aged two years, four months.	8
Mace, Miss Lottie B.	12 Jul 1881	From AuSable valley. Visiting town.	21
Mace, W.S.	28 Apr [1880]	Visiting.	15
[Mace?], Walter	29 May 1879	Played and sang at school picnic at Mace District in Clintonville.	10
[Mace], Walter	28 Apr [1880]	Tunes organs and pianos.	15
Macomber, Mr.	26 Aug 1879	From Clintonville. With daughter visited Wilmington.	12
Macomber, Miss Lillie	17 Aug [1881]	From Clintonville. She and friends were guests at Loami Bliss'.	21
Malbone, Evan	21 Apr 1881	Horse mysteriously died.	20
Markham, Clarke	1 Nov [1877]	Visiting; poor health prevents return to Wisconsin. Brother of Mrs. Tuttle of St. Lawrence.	1
Marshall, Bertha	21 Jul [1881]	Recites at village school closing ceremonies.	21
Marshall, Elmer	27 Feb 1880	Spoke at Wilmington's village school's graduation exercises.	14

Alphabetical Order by Person listed			
Name Mentioned	Date	Subject	Scrapbook Page
Marshall, Laura	27 Feb 1880	Spoke at Wilmington's village school's graduation exercises.	14
Marshall, Miss Laura	22 Oct 1879	Recited at M.E. Sunday School concert.	13
Marshall, Mr. R.	25 Apr 1878	Renting farm from Mr. Lawrence.	5
Marshall, Rollin	31 Dec 1877	Has purchased R.C. Lawrence and Herman Preston farms. Will reside on Lawrence farm in spring.	3
Marshall, Rollin	15 May [1878]	Selected Superintendent of the Sabbath School in E. Watson's district.	5
Marshall, Rollin	18 Mar [1879]	Has purchased the place formerly known as the Sampson lot.	8
Marshall, Rollin	25 Jun 1879	His runaway horse in Markhamville demolishes buggy belonging to Aaron Hays. No one hurt.	10
Marshall, Rollin	22 Oct 1879	Elected Trustee at annual school meeting for 1 year term.	13
Marshall, Rollin	14 Oct [1880]	Term as School Trustee has expired.	[17]
Marshall, Rollin	9 Mar 1881	Has the mail route for next year.	19
Marshall, Rollin	n.d. (between 9 Mar 1881 and 6 Apr 1881)	Evidently lost mail route contract.	19
Marshall, Mr. And Mrs. Rollin	Birth, n.d.	A son born to 16 Jul 1879 in Wilmington.	4

Alphabetical Order by Person listed			
Name Mentioned	Date	Subject	Scrapbook Page
Mathews, Rev. John	24 Jun [1880]	He and family guests at S.G. Williams. On way to Lake Placid for vacation.	16
Maynard, Mr.	16 Apr [1879]	Purchased farm from John Nye, who previously had purchased it from Horace Hinds.	9
Maynard, Ellen	27 Feb 1880	Spoke at Wilmington's village school's graduation exercises.	14
Maynard, Frank	21 Jul [1881]	Recites at village school closing ceremonies.	21
Maynard, Katie	9 Mar 1881	Recited at Wilmington village school closing exercises.	19
Maynard, Stella	27 Feb 1880	Spoke at Wilmington's village school's graduation exercises.	14
Maynard, Stella	9 Mar 1881	Recited at Wilmington village school closing exercises.	19
Mears, Miss Mary	Obit, n.d.	Aged 16, died at East Franklin, VT. 16 Feb 1879.	6
Merrill, Rev.	Obit, n.d.	From AuSable Forks. Officiated at funeral of Susan E. McLeod Washburn who died 10 Aug 1879.	10
Merrill, Rev. B.	Marriage, n.d.	Married Bidney Conerboy and Byron R. Brewster at AuSable Forks' American House 19 Mar 1879.	8
Merrill, Horace	22 Oct 1877	Arrested for misrepresentation, etc.	1

Alphabetical Order by Person listed			
Name Mentioned	Date	Subject	Scrapbook Page
Merrill, Horace	19 Dec 1877	A thief, but not convicted.	2
Merrill, Horace	23 Dec 1877	Arrested.	3
Merrill, Mr. I.	28 Apr [1880]	"No better."	15
Merrill, Issac	5 Jun 1879	"On complaint of his wife," jailed.	10
Merrill, Isaac	21 Apr 1880	"Quite sick."	15
Merrill, Mrs. Isaac	19 Dec 1877	Threatened by Horace Merrill.	2
Merrill, Jefferson	22 Sept 1880	Died. "An old and respected citizen of this town." Funeral tomorrow at M.E. Church.	[17]
Merrill, Mrs. John	12 Jun 1879	Lives in Omro, Wisconsin. Her niece of Wilmington is Miss Fannie Hickok.	10
Mihill, Bell	27 Feb 1880	Spoke at Wilmington's village school's graduation exercises.	14
Mihill, Beth	21 Jul [1881]	Recites at village school closing ceremonies.	20
Mihill, Dell	27 Feb 1880	Spoke at Wilmington's village school's graduation exercises.	14
Mihill, Ellen	27 Feb 1880	Spoke at Wilmington's village school's graduation exercises.	14
Mihill, F.	22 Oct 1879	Recited at M.E. Sunday School concert.	13
Mihill, Fred	27 Feb 1880	Spoke at Wilmington's village school's graduation exercises.	14

Alphabetical Order by Person listed			
Name Mentioned	Date	Subject	Scrapbook Page
Mihill, Fred	9 Mar 1881	Recited at Wilmington village school closing exercises.	19
Mihill, H.	22 Oct 1879	Recited at M.E. Sunday School concert.	13
Mihill, Henry	27 Feb 1880	Spoke at Wilmington's village school's graduation exercises.	14
Mihill, Henry	9 Mar 1881	Recited at Wilmington village school closing exercises.	19
Mihill, Kittie	27 Feb 1880	Won a spelling prize at Wilmington village school.	14
Mihill, Kittie	21 Jul [1881]	Recites (twice) at village school closing ceremonies.	21
Mihill, Miss Kittie	22 Oct 1879	Recited at M.E. Sunday School concert.	13
Mihill, Sylvester	7 Jan 1878	Has moved into village of Wilmington.	3
Mihill, Sylvester	4 Sept 1879	Purchased a lot on Plesant St. from W.F. Weston, and is building house.	12
Mihill, Sylvester	15 May 1881	Building a new house on Pleasant St.	20
Mihill, Mrs. Valentine	12 Jul 1881	Seriously ill.	21
Mihill, Wm.	5 May 1880	Saw a potato bug.	15
Mihill, Wm.	19 Apr 1881	Is painting new bridge.	19
Mihill, Mrs. Wm.	22 Oct 1877	Ill, typhoid.	1
Mihill, Mr. and Mrs. Wm.	12 Jun 1879	Visiting Henry Avery at Wadhams Mills.	10

Alphabetical Order by Person listed			
Name Mentioned	Date	Subject	Scrapbook Page
Miles, Mr.	25 Apr 1878	Moving into a part of Wm. Bell's house.	5
Miles, John	Death, n.d.	Died, aged 72 years, in Wilmington 14 Jan 1878.	3
Miles, John	15 Jan 1878	"Old and respected" Wilmington resident who died last week. Member of Presbyterian Church. Leaves a widow.	3
Miles, Joseph	21 Apr 1880	"Has taken the Cole farm."	15
Miles, Joseph	10 Dec 1880	"Low with consumption."	[17]
Miller, Joseph	25 Apr 1878	Until recently had occupied Hiram Patridge farm.	5
Morhous, Mr. C.	2 Jan [1879]	From Saranac Lake; visiting friends.	7
Morhous, Charles	27 Jan 1881	From Saranac Lakes. In town.	18
Mustgrove, Mr.	21 Apr 1881	From Black Brook. Funeral for at Weston school house, Wed. 20 Apr 1881.	20
Nash, Carrie A.	Marriage, n.d.	From North Elba. On 1 Jan 1878 marries Fred. Lamb of North Elba at Wilmington's Congregational Parsonage by Rev. T. Watson.	8
Naylor, Miss Nellie J.	Marriage, n.d.	From Keene. Married David Nye of Keene 20 Mar 1879 at M.E. Parsonage of Upper Jay by Rev. G.H. VanDusen.	8

Alphabetical Order by Person listed			
Name Mentioned	Date	Subject	Scrapbook Page
Negus, Rev.	15 Jan 1878	Jay Baptist minister preaches at Wilmington M.E. Church.	3
Nye, Mr.	14 Jul 1880	Owns a store?	16
Nye, Mr.	12 Nov 1877	Visiting Malone.	1
Nye, Mr. C.F.	18 Mar [1880]	From Keene. Visits Wilmington.	14
Nye, Mrs. C.F.	24 Jun [1880]	From Keene. Visiting.	16
Nye, Mr. and Mrs. C.F.	30 Mar 1880	From Keene. Attended church in Wilmington.	14
Nye, Mr. and Mrs. Daniel	21 Jul [1881]	From Keene. Attended church in Wilmington.	21
Nye, David	Marriage, n.d.	From Keene. Married Miss Nellie J. Nylor of Keene 20 Mar 1879 at M.E. Parsonage of Upper Jay by Rev. G.H. VanDusen.	8
Nye, Master Horace	17 Dec 1879	Is assisting as a clerk his brother John in W.F. Weston's store.	13
Nye, Miss Ida	15 May 1881	From Jay. Teaching in the E. Weston district.	20
Nye, Jasper	21 Jul [1881]	Recites at village school closing ceremonies.	21
Nye, John	22 Oct 1877	Sabbath School recital.	1
Nye, John	13 Feb 1878	Has bought William Mihill's house and lot in Wilmington village. Latest of several purchases.	3
Nye, John	21 May [1878]	Chosen Treasurer of Wilmington M.E. Church Sabbath School.	5

Alphabetical Order by Person listed			
Name Mentioned	Date	Subject	Scrapbook Page
Nye, John	16 Apr [1879]	Has bought Horace Hinds farm, instead of R.C. Lawrence's. Nye then sold it to Mr. Maynard.	9
Nye, John	21 May 1879	The Secretary of M.E. Church Sabbath School.	10
[Nye], John	17 Dec 1879	Clerks in W.F. Weston's store.	13
Nye, John	18 Mar [1880]	Bought an organ.	14
Nye, John	7 Aug [1880]	Purchased an organ from J.E. Everett.	16
Nye, John	16 Apr 1881	His majority for Supervisor was 28, not 14.	19
Nye, John	15 May 1881	Sold house and lot to Cassius Winch.	20
Nye, Mrs. John	12 May [1880]	Humorous story about a cat who suckles baby rat.	15
Nye, Mr. and Mrs. John	10 Jul 1879	Visited friends at Mechum Lake.	11
Nye, Mr. and Mrs. John, Miss Lila and Master Jasper	26 Aug 1879	All of Wilmington, together with Mrs. F.M. Parker of St. Albans, visited Keene, etc.	12
Nye, John W.	2 Mar 1881	Elected Wilmington Town Supervisor "by a good majority."	18
Nye, Lila	27 Feb 1880	Spoke at Wilmington's village school's graduation exercises.	14
Nye, Lila	21 Jul [1881]	Recites (twice) at village school closing ceremonies.	21
Nye, Percival	31 Dec 1877	Has just wed Adda Benedict.	3

Alphabetical Order by Person listed			
Name Mentioned	Date	Subject	Scrapbook Page
Nye, Mr. and Mrs. Wells	16 Apr 1881	From Jay. Guests of John Nye.	19
O'Brien, Miss B.	6 Mar [1879]	From AuSable Forks. Visiting her sister in Wilmington.	8
O'Brien, Mr. and Mrs. Hugh	Births, n.d.	On Palmer Hill a son born to 7 Mar 1880.	14
Olney, Mrs.	13 Dec 1877	Recovered from illness.	2
Olney, Nelly	5 Dec 1877	She and 3 children visiting in Jay and Wilmington. She is daughter of Jasper Bliss.	2
O'Neil, Miss Mary	17 Jun [1881]	Drowned on way to teach at V. Bartlett's. Daughter of Ned O'Neil, formerly of Wilmington, sister of the late Thomas. Father, sister and brother survive her.	20
O'Neil, Miss Mary	22 Jun [1881]	Funeral held for at AuSable Forks Catholic Church. Rev. Father Fitzgerald officiated.	20
O'Neil, Ned	25 Apr 1878	Sold his farm to R.C. Lawrence.	5
O'Neil, Ned	17 Jun [1881]	Father of Mary, who recently drowned; of Thomas who drowned 2 years ago in May; and of another son and daughter. Formerly of Wilmington.	20
O'Neil, Patsey	9 May 1879	Hired by Henry Van Hoevenbergh of New York.	9

Alphabetical Order by Person listed			
Name Mentioned	Date	Subject	Scrapbook Page
O'Neil, Thomas	9 May 1879	Killed while driving logs on Schroon River on Wed [May 7]. Father lives in Keene. Services in AuSable Forks.	9
O'Neil, Thomas	17 Jun [1881]	He drowned 2 years ago in May. Father is Ned O'Neil, formerly of Wilmington. A sister named Mary, and also a brother and another sister.	20
O'Neill, E.	4 Jun 1879 Indian Carry, NY	Father of Thomas G. O'Neill.	0
O'Neill, Mary	4 Jun 1879 Indian Carry, NY	Sister of Thomas G. O'Neill.	0
O'Neill, Thomas G.	4 Jun 1879 Indian Carry, NY	Poetic obit. for, died May 1879.	0
Ornsby, Mrs. Sarah	12 Nov 1877	Formerly of Wilmington, now of Boston, for a year committed in Concord insane asylum, has regained her reason. Her nephews; Charles Williams of Elizabethtown, G.G. Williams of Wilmington.	1
Owen, Miss Anna	15 May 1881	Gone to Nyack, NY, for the season.	20
Owen, Elmer	9 Mar 1881	Recited at Wilmington village school closing exercises.	19

Alphabetical Order by Person listed

Name Mentioned	Date	Subject	Scrapbook Page
Owen, Miss Emma	10 Jul 1879	From Oshkosh, WI. She has resided for last 9 years in the West. Visiting friends in Wilmington with her sister Mrs. Melvin Wardner of Keeseville.	11
Owen, Ida	5 Dec 1877	Will attend school at North Elba.	2
Owen, Miss Ida	Marriage, n.d.	From AuSable Chasm. On 1 Jan 1879 marries Leroy Gaskell of Clintonville. Married in Peru at M.E. Parsonage by Rev. Lewis.	8
Owen, Miss Ida	22 Oct 1877	In school Lyceum.	1
Owen, Isaac	Deaths, n.d.	Died in Wilmington 12 Aug 1880, aged 72 years.	16
Owen, Isaac	13 Aug 1880	Funeral services for. Was 72. "An old and highly esteemed resident" of Wilmington. Was a member of Congregational Church.	16
Owen, Mr. and Mrs. Orlin	Birth, n.d.	A daughter born to Nov 1877 in Chicago, Illinois.	2
Parker, Mrs. F.M.	26 Aug 1879	From St. Albans. With her son, and the John Nye family of Wilmington, she visited Keene, etc.	12

Alphabetical Order by Person listed			
Name Mentioned	Date	Subject	Scrapbook Page
Parkhurst, Mr. H.S.	6 Aug [1879]	A prominent lawyer from Gloversville, who with Col. H.A. Hascall, and their wives, are guests of Hon. W.F. Weston.	11
Patridge, Hiram	25 Apr 1878	Sold his farm to R.C. Lawrence.	5
Perry, Mr. A.	23 Jan 1878	A burn victim, he is doing better.	3
Perry, Alpheus	15 Jan 1878	Kerosene lamp exploded at his place.	3
Perry, Alpheus	4 Jul [1878]	House burns; family ok but looses everything; he is 80 miles away at work.	6
Perry, Mr. and Mrs. George	Birth, n.d.	A daughter born to 12 Feb 1878 in Wilmington.	2
Perry, Mr. M.	18 Apr [1879]	From Black Brook. A bear scared his granddaughter in sugar woods.	9
Perry, Mrs. W.	22 Oct 1879	Sang at M.E. Sunday School concert.	13
Perry, Wm.	30 Mar 1880	He and family moved to Lewis.	14
Petit, Mr.	13 Nov [1880]	Pall bearer at funeral of Mrs. Kemp, mother of E.S. Kemp, at AuSable Forks Episcopal Church.	[17]
Pierce, Mr.	13 Nov [1880]	Pall bearer at funeral of Mrs. Kemp, mother of E.S. Kemp, at AuSable Forks Episcopal Church.	[17]
Pillsbury, Mr. and N.	22 Oct 1879	From Ohio. Visiting friends. Mrs. is daughter of R. Hickok	13

Alphabetical Order by Person listed			
Name Mentioned	Date	Subject	Scrapbook Page
Powers, Alice Miss	Obit, n.d.	Aged 23 years, died of consumption 3 Oct 1878 at Abbott's Corner, Canada.	4
Preston, Miss Addie	Marriage, n.d.	Married McDonald Lamoy in Jay 29 Jun 1879 by Rev. J. McKernon. Both bride and groom reside in Wilmington.	5
Preston, Mr. and Mrs. Carlos	Birth, n.d.	A son born to, in Wilmington, 4 Sept 1878.	5
Preston, Elijah	11 Sept 1879	His 2 sisters from St. Lawrence Co. visiting.	12
Preston, Elijah	13 Feb [1880]	"A little daughter" of his, broke her arm.	14
Preston, Elijah	9 Jun 1880	Has the agency for Warner's patent washer.	15
Preston, Mr. And Mrs. Elijah	Obit, n.d.	Their daughter Mrs. Peter Soloman died of fits.	7
Preston, Herman	31 Dec 1877	Sold his farm to Rollin Marshall. Is excellent citizen.	3
Preston, Melvin	13 Jan 1880	Nearly died from cut foot.	18
Quirk, Mr.	27 Jan 1881 AuSable Forks	Teaches at AuSable Forks' School.	18
Quirk, M.H.	22 Sept 1880	From AuSable Forks. Addressed the Democratic meeting at Markhamville.	[17]
Reed, Mr.	12 Nov 1877	Rents Mr. Gorman's hotel in AuSable Forks.	1
Reeves, Mrs. Ada	26 Mar 1879	With [her father] R. Hickok is visiting friends in Bloomingdale.	9

Alphabetical Order by Person listed			
Name Mentioned	Date	Subject	Scrapbook Page
Revitte, Dr. F.A.	21 Feb [1880]	Attending to Henry Hinds.	14
Richardson, Mrs.	25 Mar 1878	"Recovering."	4
Rivit, Dr.	22 Mar 1878	Dr. from AuSable Forks.	4
Robbins, Rev.	21 Apr [1881]	From Chazy. Delivered sermon at M.E. Church.	21
Robinson, Mr.	22 Mar 1878	Played music at Wilmington M.E. Church.	4
Rogers, Esq. James	Deaths, n.d.	Conducted funeral at Adirondack House on Sat. for Roy, son of Mr. And Mrs. E.S. Kemp, who died 14 May 1880.	15
Rowe, Mrs.	24 Aug 1878	She and daughter have returned home to Plattsburgh.	6
Ruffner, Vivion W.	Marriages, n.d.	Marries in Essex 28 Jul 1879 at the residence of her grandfather, Noble Clemons, Miss Nellie Shumway. United in marriage by Rev. E.L. Troy, Pastor of St. John's Church. Bride and groom both from Chicago.	9
Russel, Mary	9 Mar 1881	Recited at Wilmington village school closing exercises.	19
Russell, ___	19 Dec 1877	Victim of theft by Horace Merrill.	2
Russell, Mr.	5 Dec 1877	Theft of his property.	2
Russell, Mr.	30 Jul 1879	His haying bee attended by 26 mowers.	11

Alphabetical Order by Person listed			
Name Mentioned	Date	Subject	Scrapbook Page
Russell, Eddie	13 Feb [1880]	Severely cut his foot.	14
Russell, Mrs. Ella	21 Jul [1881]	From Keene. In town.	21
Russell, Martin	12 Jul 1881	"Quite sick."	20
Sanders, H.	4 Sept 1879	H. and family have returned from White Mountains.	12
Sanders, Henry	16 Apr 1881	His "team" of horses died unexpectedly.	19
Sanford, Dr. J.	6 Aug [1879]	From Castleton, VT. With A. Mace of AuSable, visitingRupert's family	11
Sawyer, Dr.	20 Apr 1878	Dr. from AuSable Forks.	4
Sawyer, Dr.	27 Jan 1881 (AuSable Forks)	Attending cases of croup.	18
Sears, Mrs. William	30 Apr [1879]	The granddaughter of Wesley Galusha, lives in Sutton Falls, P.Q.	9
Severence, Charles	9 Jun 1880	From Lewis. Together with Edwin Hays and family of Stowers' forge, visiting Aaron Hays.	15
Shaubutt, Rev.	5 Dec 1877	Officiates at funeral.	2
Sheldon, Nelson	Marriages, n.d.	Married Miss Hannah Hickok 12 Mar 1881 at Wilmington's Congregational Parsonage. Married by Rev. Thomas Watson. Both of Wilmington.	19
Sheldon, Mr. and Mrs. Nelson	n.d. (between 9 Mar and 6 Apr 1881)	Have moved to VT.	19

Alphabetical Order by Person listed			
Name Mentioned	Date	Subject	Scrapbook Page
Shields, Rev. Father	22 Mar 1878	From AuSable Forks. Delivered address on Popes.	4
Shumway, Ambrose	Obit, n.d.	Aged 74, died 1 Apr 1878 in Wilmington.	4
Shumway, Charles	30 Jul 1879	Received a pension check for $2600.	11
Shumway, Miss Nellie	Marriage, n.d.	In Essex 28 Jul 1879 at home of her grandfather, Noble Clemons, Rev. E.L. Troy Pastor of St. John's Church unites her in marriage to Vivion W. Ruffner, both of Chicago.	9
Shumway, Peter	16 Jun 1880	Renting R.C. Lawrence's "Pay Place."	16
Shumway, Peter	23 Dec 1880	"A little stranger has made it's appearance at [his] home."	[17]
Silter, S.	22 Oct 1877	In school Lyceum.	1
Slater, George	9 Mar 1881	Recited at Wilmington village school closing exercises.	19
Slater, Mr. J.	17 Aug [1881]	Received a pension of $900.	21
Slater, Mr. and Mrs. N.B.	27 Jan 1881 (AuSable Forks)	Gone to Lewis to visit friends.	18
Slater, Mr. S.	9 Mar 1881	Elected Chairman of group to raise funds via an exhibition for a church organ stool and chandeliers.	19
Slatter, Sammy	22 Mar 1878	Acted in play at Wilmington M.E. Church.	4

Alphabetical Order by Person listed			
Name Mentioned	Date	Subject	Scrapbook Page
Smith, Mr. and Mrs. (and family)	29 Aug 1878	From Philadelphia. Attends M.E. Church and Mr. Smith preaches at Congregational Church.	6
Smith, Charley	19 Apr 1881	From Upper Jay. The new bridge in Wilmington is "under [his] supervision."	19
Smith, Henry	Deaths, n.d.	Son of Henry and Margurite Smith died 14 Sept 1880 in Wilmington. Aged 10 years.	16
Smith, Joseph	31 Dec 1877	Gave a temperance recital at Lucena Estes' school.	3
Smith, Joseph	13 Jan 1881	He and family returned to West.	18
Smith, Joseph	21 Apr 1881	"Dangerously ill."	20
Smith, Mr. and Mrs. Joseph	Birth, n.d.	A son born to 18 Jan 1878 in Wilmington.	2
Smith, Rev. Levi S.	Marriage, n.d.	Married at Middle Granville 10 Dec 1879 Edward W. Harringan of Comstocks and Miss Minnie L. White, daughter of Geo. C. White of Middle White, and granddaughter of the late Peter Comstock of Port Kent.	11
Smith, Luke	21 May 1879	Two "large bears" in his garden.	10
Smith, Luke	4 Nov [1880]	Lost a horse.	[17]

Alphabetical Order by Person listed			
Name Mentioned	Date	Subject	Scrapbook Page
Smith, Walter	1 Apr [1879]	From Markhamville. Dangerously ill with canker rash.	9
Soloman, Mrs. Peter	Obit, n.d.	Of Saranac Lakes. Daughter of Mr. And Mrs. Elijah Preston. Died of "fits," on Tues.	7
Spafford, Mrs. Wm.	11 Sept 1879	From Plattsburgh. Visiting with Miss Emma Lansing of Plattsburgh, and formerly of Wilmington.	12
Sterns, Charles	25 Jun 1879	Has store in Keeseville. Sold hall carpet.	10
Stevens, George	14 Jul 1880	From North Elba. In town.	16
Stevens, Henry	21 Apr 1881	From North Elba. Sold a fine horse to Edmond Bliss.	20
Stevens, Henry	15 May 1881	"Has taken the Notch House, and has a fair prospect of a full house during the sporting season."	20
Stevens, Mr. and Mrs. Henry	2 Mar 1881	They and son, from Burlington, VT, guests at Loamie Bliss'.	18
Stevens, Mr. and Mrs. Henry	5 May 1881	A daughter born to 15 Jun 1881 in Wilmington, at Notch House.	20
Stevens, J.	17 Jul 1879	From North Elba. In hotel business.	11
Stevenson, Mrs. Thomas	17 Dec 1879	"Dangerously ill."	13
Stevenson, Wm.	30 Mar 1880	His daughter adopted by Mr. And Mrs. Sanford Avery	14

Alphabetical Order by Person listed			
Name Mentioned	Date	Subject	Scrapbook Page
Stevenson, William	4 Nov [1880]	Receiving a pension of $1500.	[17]
Stickney, Daniel	29? Aug 1880	From Jay. He and his sister, Mrs. E. Jucket, of Poultney, V.T., are guests of John Hinds.	16
Storr, Mr.	26 Jun 1878	Theft of barrel of pork.	6
Storrs, Eva	7 Aug [1880]	Entertaining guests.	16
Storrs, Miss Eva	6 Apr 1881	Teaching at Duane.	19
Storrs, Miss Eva	21 Jul [1881]	Home from Duane.	21
Storrs, Hat	7 Aug [1880]	Entertaining guests.	16
Storrs, Miss Hat	13 Feb [1880]	Her school in Markhamville closes, with "spelling school."	14
Storrs, Miss Hattie	26 Nov 1879	Teaching at Markhamville.	13
Storrs, Miss Hattie	5 May 1880	Teaching on Alstead Hill.	15
Storrs, Mrs. I.H.	4 Sept 1879	"Is gaining slowly."	12
Storrs, Ira	7 Jan 1878	Has house on road leading to the Upper Forge.	3
Storrs, Ira	25 Apr 1878	Will remodel house to take in Summer boarders.	5
Storrs, Ira	14 Aug 1878	Convicted and fined for "selling intoxicating beverages."	6
Storrs, Ira	n.d. (between 9 Mar and 6 Apr 1881)	His run away team killed one of Sanford Avery's sheep.	19

Alphabetical Order by Person listed			
Name Mentioned	Date	Subject	Scrapbook Page
Storrs, Ira	5 May 1881	Horse died.	20
Storrs, Mrs. Ira	12 Jun 1879	Very ill, but better.	10
Storrs, Mrs. Ira	30 Jul 1879	Had a relapse. Dangerously ill.	11
Storrs, Mrs. Ira	13 Aug [1879]	Has improved.	11
Storrs, Mrs. Ira	10 Dec 1879	"Quite sick again."	13
Storrs, Mrs. Ira	5 May 1880	"Quite sick again."	15
Storrs, Mrs. Ira	21 Apr 1881	"Very low again."	20
Sumner, Mr. And Mrs. H.	23 Jan 1878	From Upper Jay. Attends church service in Wilmington.	3
Taylor, Mr.	13 Jan 1881	"Are spending a few days in Clintonville."	18
Taylor, Miss Abba	Marriages, n.d.	From North Elba. Marries Herbert E. Hinds 16 Oct 1879. Married in Wilmington by Rev. Thomas Watsen.	11
Taylor, Rev. Wm. M.	20 Nov [1877]	"Sermon published by."	1
Thayer, A.Q.	22 Mar 1878	Acted in play at Wilmington M.E. Church.	4
Thayer, A.Q.	27 Feb 1880	From Wilmington. An adult who spoke at Wilmington village school graduation.	14
Thayer, Banney	4 Nov [1880]	Teaching in North Elba.	[17]
Thayer, Charles	n.d. (between 9 Mar and 6 Apr 1881)	Has mail route for coming season, not Rollin Marshall.	19

Alphabetical Order by Person listed			
Name Mentioned	Date	Subject	Scrapbook Page
Thayer, Charles	5 May 1881	One of his oxen died.	20
Thayer, Mrs. Charles	22 Oct 1877	Sabbath School recital.	1
Thayer, Mrs. Charles	22 Oct 1879	Recited at M.E. Sunday School concert.	13
Thayer, Colvin	22 Mar 1878	Acted in play at Wilmington M.E. Church.	4
Thayer, Corwin	22 Mar 1878	Directed play at Wilmington M.E. Church.	4
Thayer, Corwin	2 Mar 1881	Studying law in Elizabethtown. Home on a visit.	18
Thayer, Mrs. E.	17 Jul 1879	Superintendent of Markhamville Sabbath School.	11
Thayer, Eddie	9 Mar 1881	Recited at Wilmington village school closing exercises.	19
Thayer, Elijah	13 Jun [1878]	Chosen Superintendent of Sabbath School in Markhamville.	5
Thayer, Mrs. Elijah	13 Sept 1878	Markhamville's Sabbath School Superintendent; a picnic.	7
Thayer, Mrs. Illijah	20 Nov [1877]	Taught Sabbath School in Markhamville.	1
Thayer, Etta	9 Mar 1881	Recited at Wilmington school closing exercises.	19
Thayer, Leonard	22 Mar 1878	Acted in play at Wilmington M.E. Church.	4
Thayer, Moses	9 Mar 1881	Recited at Wilmington school closing exercises.	19

Alphabetical Order by Person listed			
Name Mentioned	Date	Subject	Scrapbook Page
Thompson, Mr. and Mrs. Charley	4 Sept 1879	From Winooski Falls VT. Together with Mrs. E. Fox of Brooklyn NY, and Mrs. E.S. Kemp of AuSable Forks were guests of J. Hinds.	12
Thrasher, Prof.	22 Jun [1881]	Lectured on phrenology, and has started a writing school.	20
Torrence, Master	17 Aug [1881]	With Master Baldwin, both of AuSable Forks, in town buying fat cattle.	21
Torrence, Anna	9 Mar 1881	Recited at Wilmington village school closing services.	19
Torrence, Anna	21 Jul [1881]	Recites at village school closing ceremonies.	21
Torrence, Eugene	27 Feb 1880	Spoke at Wilmington's village school's graduation exercises.	14
Torrence, Eugene	9 Mar 1881	Recited at Wilmington village school closing exercises.	19
Torrence, J.	22 Oct 1879	Recited at M.E. Sunday School concert.	13
Troy, Rev. E.L.	Marriages, n.d.	Pastor of St. John's Church marries in Essex 28 Jul 1879 Miss Nellie Shumway and Vivion W Ruffner, both of Chicago.	9
Truman, Mrs. Joshua	13 Jan 1881	Truman, Mrs. Joshua has consumption. Spent 3 months at her father's. Has returned home to die.	18
Trumbull, Mr. and Mrs. John	Births, n.d.	A daughter born to 9 Feb 1881 in AuSable Forks.	18

Alphabetical Order by Person listed

Name Mentioned	Date	Subject	Scrapbook Page
Tuttle, Mrs.	1 Nov [1877]	Visiting from St. Lawrence; sister of Clarke Markham.	1
Vanderwaker	25 Mar 1878	A family, perhaps no longer resident, in Wilmington: the Vanderwaker's house burned.	4
Vanderwaker, Mrs. Isaac	5 Dec 1877	Died from a "fit of apoplexy" in Markhamville at home of Mr. Benham, her son-in-law.	2
VanDusen, Rev. G.H.	Marriage, n.d.	Married David Nye and Miss Nellie J. Naylor, both of Keene, 20 Mar 1879 at M.E. Parsonage in Upper Jay.	8
Vennor	13 Feb [1880]	Weather predictor.	14
Wardner, Alfred	17 Aug [1881]	Wed Miss Phebe Hays.	21
Wardner, Charley	22 Mar 1878	Acted in play at Wilmington M.E. Church.	4
Wardner, Charley	24 Nov [1880]	Purchased Nathan Wardner farm.	[17]
Wardner, Mrs. Melvin	10 Jul 1879	From Keeseville. She and her sister Miss Emma Owen of Oshkosh, WI, are visiting.	11
Wardner, Rev. N.	20 Nov [1877]	From Chazy. Preached in Wilmington.	1
Wardner, Rev. N.	12 Mar 1879	From Chazy. Gave sermon at Wilmington's M.E. Church.	8

Alphabetical Order by Person listed			
Name Mentioned	Date	Subject	Scrapbook Page
Wardner, Nathan	24 Nov [1880]	Sold his house to Charley Wardner.	[17]
Wardner, Seth	26 Nov [1877]	Lives in Bloomingdale, evidently with sister.	2
Wardner, Mr. and Mrs. Seth	8 May 1878	"Young bride and groom" from Bloomingdale visited friends in town 2 weeks ago.	5
Wardner, Mr. and Mrs. Seth	26 Jun 1878	From Bloomingdale; attend Wilmington church.	6
Wardner, Mr. and Mrs. Seth	12 Nov [1879]	From Bloomingdale. Visiting.	13
Wardner, Mr. and Mrs. Seth	2 Mar 1881	From Bloomingdale. In town.	18
Wardner, William	13 Sept 1878	His "young people" picking raspberries and strawberries.	7
Wardner, William	6 Apr 1881	Has bought the Smith Harris farm.	19
Wardner, Mrs. William	2 Mar 1881	Spent a few weeks in Bloomingdale. Now home.	18
Washburn, J.G.	Obit, n.d.	Husband of Susan E. McLeod Washburn, who died 10 Aug 1879.	10

Alphabetical Order by Person listed

Name Mentioned	Date	Subject	Scrapbook Page
Washburn, Susan E. McLeod	Obit, n.d.	Died 10 Aug 1879 of heart disease in Wilmington, aged 43 years. Wife of J.G. Washburn. Daughter of Jefferson McLeod. Funeral held at Markhamville with Revs. Thomas Watson of Wilmington and Merrill of AuSable Forks officiating, and funeral conducted by Mr. FitzGerald of Black Brook.	10
Washer, J.	30 Jul 1879	Sold a Meadow King Mower to David Hazelton.	11
Washer, Mr. J.	25 Jun 1879	From Clintonville. An agent for the Meadow King Mowing Machine. Evidently visited Rupert's home.	10
Watsen, Rev. Thomas	Marriages, n.d.	Married Herbert E. Hinds of Wilmington, and Miss Abba Taylor of North Elba at Wilmington 16 Oct 1879.	11
Watson, Arthur	27 Feb 1880	Spoke at Wilmington's village school's graduation exercises.	14
Watson, Arthur	6 Apr 1881	Clerking for W.F. Weston.	19
Watson, David	25 Jan 1880	"Injured while splitting cedar posts."	13

Alphabetical Order by Person listed

Name Mentioned	Date	Subject	Scrapbook Page
Watson, Rev. T.	Marriage, n.d.	Marries couple at Wilmington's Congregational Parsonage 6 Aug 1878.	5
Watson, Rev. T.	Marriage, n.d.	Marries Ira B. Lyon and Addie L. Lewis 31 Dec 1878 at Wilmington's Congregational Parsonage.	8
Watson, Rev. T.	Marriage, n.d.	Marries Carrie A. Nash and Fred Lamb 1 Jan 1878 at Wilmington's Congregational Parsonage.	8
Watson, Rev. T.	21 Apr 1881	From Wilmington. Officiated, together with Rev. Harmon from Jay, at Mrs. Frank Jordan's funeral at Wilmington's Congregational Church, 9 Apr 1881.	20
Watson, Mrs. Thomas	3 Apr 1878	Quite ill.	4
Watson, Mrs. Thomas	29 Aug 1878	Has been quite ill of heart disease, but improving.	6
Watson, Mrs. Thomas	12 Feb 1879	Very ill with heart disease.	8
Watson, Mrs. Thomas	25 Jan 1880	"Sick with heart disease."	13
Watson, Mr. and Mrs. Thomas	Birth, n.d.	A son born to 12 Apr 1878 in Wilmington.	4
Watson, Rev. Thomas	Marriages, n.d.	Married Onias Wilkins and Miss Rose Haselton, both of Wilmington, at Wilmington's Congregational Parsonage 6 Dec 1879.	11

Alphabetical Order by Person listed			
Name Mentioned	Date	Subject	Scrapbook Page
Watson, Rev. Thomas	Marriages, n.d.	Married Miss Hannah Hickok and Nelson Sheldon at Wilmington's Congregational Parsonage 12 Mar 1881.	19
Watson, Rev. Thomas	Obit, n.d.	Officiates at Mrs. John S. Hinds' funeral.	7
Watson, Rev. Thomas	Obit, n.d.	From Wilmington. Officiated at funeral of Susan E. McLeod Washburn, who died 10 Aug 1879.	10
Watson, Rev. Thomas	5 Dec 1877	Officiates at funeral.	2
Watson, Rev. Thomas	6 Mar [1879]	Donation for the pastor taken at his church, Congregational Church at Wilmington.	8
Watson, Rev. Thomas	16 Jun 1880	Engaged for another year at Congregational Church	16
Watson, Rev. Thomas	24 Jun [1880]	Pastor of Congregational Church.	16
Watson, Rev. Thomas	22 Sept 1880	Delivered remarks at Sunday School picnic, as did Rev. E.J. McKernan.	[17]
Weller, Mr. and Mrs. F.	7 Jan 1878	From Brighton. Visited Keeseville, now Wilmington.	3
Wells, Mr. and Mrs.	17 Jul 1879	From Shelburn, VT are visiting their daughter Mrs. W.F. Weston.	11
Wells, Miss Hattie	24 Nov [1880]	Form Frelighsburg, P.Q. Is on her first visit to New York.	[17]

Alphabetical Order by Person listed			
Name Mentioned	Date	Subject	Scrapbook Page
Wells, Miss Hattie	27 Jan 1881 AuSable Forks	From Frelighsburg, P.Q. Has been at Adirondack House for 8 weeks. Headed home.	18
Weston & Co.	19 Dec 1877	"Buying large quantities of wood."	2
W.F. Weston & Co.	25 Jan 1880	Iron works, with forge, bellows house and kilns.	13
W.F. Weston store	17 Dec 1879	Horace Nye of Keene, assisting his brother John	13
Weston and Hall	16 Dec 1878	Loss of logs due to freshet.	7
Weston, Mr.	26 Jun 1878	Stolen barrel of pork hidden in his coal pile, but discovered.	6
Weston, Aaron	11 Sept 1879	From Port Henry. In town.	12
Weston, Charles	17 Jul 1879	He and daughter, from Keeseville, are visiting friends.	11
Weston, E.	21 May [1878]	E. Weston School District.	5
Weston, E.	14 Aug 1878	E. Weston School District.	6
Weston, Eddie	9 Jun 1880	From Port Henry. Visiting friends.	15
Weston, Elijah	22 Oct 1877	Sabbath School recital.	1
Weston, Elijah	31 Dec 1877	A school district is named after.	3
Weston, Elijah	31 Dec 1877	Has repaired his house.	3
Weston, Elijah	1 Jul [1879]	Horse and wagon accident injuries.	10
Weston, Elijah	14 Jul 1880	On Wilmington's committee on building.	16
Weston, Justice Elijah	23 Dec 1877	Justice of the Peace.	3

Alphabetical Order by Person listed

Name Mentioned	Date	Subject	Scrapbook Page
Weston, G.W.	13 Sept 1878	From Port Henry; has married.	7
Weston, George	13 Jun [1878]	From Port Henry; spoke to Sabbath School.	5
Weston, Sidney	12 Mar 1879	Son of W.F. Weston. Is ill with croup.	8
Weston, Sidney	2 Mar 1881	He and son, from Winooski VT. In town.	18
Weston, Mr. Sidney	11 Sept 1879	From Winooski Falls, VT. In town.	12
Weston, Vernon	28 Apr [1880]	"Gave a birthday party."	15
Weston, Vernon	9 Jun 1880	Teaching in the North district.	15
Weston, Vernon	15 Sept 1880	Attending school at Elizabethtown.	[17]
Weston, Vernon	21 Jul [1881]	Returned from school in Elizabethtown.	21
Weston, W.F.	15 Jan 1878	Lost a horse.	3
Weston, W.F.	1 Mar 1878	150 attended fundraising ($35.75) at Weston home, evidently to support M.E. Minister.	4
Weston, W.F.	3 Apr 1878	Bought Mr. S.G. Williams flock of 41 sheep for $164.	4
Weston, W.F.	25 Apr 1878	Has "new spring goods."	5
Weston, W.F.	21 May [1878]	Chosen Secretary of Wilmington M.E. Church Sabbath School.	5
Weston, W.F.	16 Dec 1878	Bought David Hays village house.	7

Alphabetical Order by Person listed			
Name Mentioned	Date	Subject	Scrapbook Page
Weston, W.F.	15 Jan [1879]	Returned from Albany where he had a good reception. Will start forge when ore from Keene arrives.	7
Weston, W.F.	12 Feb 1879	Theft of his corn.	8
Weston, W.F.	12 Mar 1879	Has returned from Albany.	8
Weston, W.F.	18 Mar [1879]	"Preparing to draw ore from Keene, and will soon start the forge."	8
Weston, W.F.	26 Mar 1879	Mr. Hammond will manage his farm during coming year.	9
Weston, W.F.	4 Sept 1879	Sold a lot on Plesant Street to Sylvester Mihill.	12
Weston, W.F.	25 Jan 1880	8-10,000 bushels of coal lost to fire.	13
Weston, W.F.	11 Apr 1880	Two bridges over his kilns burned. Loss of $200.	14
Weston, W.F.	21 Apr 1880	Has new kilns, to be run by Zach Lawrence.	15
Weston, W.F.	28 Apr [1880]	Employed many men to drive cordwood down the river from North Elba.	15
Weston, W.F.	12 May [1880]	Humorous story about a cat who suckles baby rat.	15
Weston, W.F.	12 May [1880]	Has ca. 800 cords of wood in river.	15
Weston, W.F.	19 May 1880	Large amount of coal belonging to Mr. Conger, to be shipped to his forge, burned.	15

Alphabetical Order by Person listed

Name Mentioned	Date	Subject	Scrapbook Page
Weston, W.F.	16 Jun 1880	Large amount of coal made and drawn to his forge.	16
Weston, W.F.	8 Jul 1880	His "new kilns on the mountain are finished and ready for business."	16
Weston, W.F.	27 Jan 1881	Brick being drawn to North Elba for his new kilns.	18
Weston, W.F.	23 Feb [1881]	His "[forge] business here is progressing lively."	18
Weston, W.F.	6 Apr 1881	Thurlow Bell and Arthur Watson clerking for.	19
Weston, Hon. W.F.	6 Aug [1879]	H.S. Parkhurst of Gloversville, Col. H.A. Hascall U.S. Army, and their wives, are his guests.	11
Weston, Mr. W.F.	19 Apr 1881	Went fishing with Mr. L. Bliss up the river. "Not a bite."	19
Weston, Mrs. W.F.	22 Oct 1877	Has traveled to Burlington.	1
Weston, Mrs. W.F.	13 Dec 1877	Made a gift for Rev. R.J. Davies.	2
Weston, Mrs. W.F.	13 Dec 1877	Spent holidays with friends in VT.	2
Weston, Mrs. W.F.	25 Jun 1879	She and guests at Lake Placid.	10
Weston, Mrs. W.F.	17 Jul 1879	Her parents, Mr. And Mrs. Wells, are visiting from Shelburn, VT.	11
Weston, Mrs. W.F.	22 Oct 1879	Sang at M.E. Sunday School concert.	13
Weston, Mrs. W.F.	17 Dec 1879	Gone to VT for holidays.	13

Alphabetical Order by Person listed			
Name Mentioned	Date	Subject	Scrapbook Page
Weston, Mrs. W.F.	5 May 1881	Gone to visit friends in VT.	20
Weston, Mr. and Mrs. W.F.	12 Jun 1879	Visited by "The Honorable Clerk of Assembly and family."	10
Weston, Mr. and Mrs. W.F.	13 Aug [1879]	Guests at Lake Placid.	11
Weston, Mr. and Mrs. W.F.	25 Sept 1879	Returned from Saratoga.	12
Weston, Mr. and Mrs. W.F.	4 Aug 1881	Mr. And Mrs. William Weston of Winooski, VT visiting.	21
Weston, Warren	22 Oct 1877	Sabbath School recital.	1
Weston, Warren	6 Nov 1877	Hunting trip to Lake Placid.	1
Weston, Mr. and Mrs. William	4 Aug 1881	From Winooski, VT. Guests of Mr. and Mrs. W.F. Weston	21
White, Geo. C.	Marriages, n.d.	From Middle Granville. His daughter, Miss Minnie L. White marries Edward W. Harringan of Comstock 10 Dec 1879 at Middle Granville. Geo.'s mother was probably a Comstock, Minnie's grandfather is the late Peter Comstock of Port Kent.	11
White, George C.	7 Jan 1878	From Plattsburgh. Visiting in Wilmington.	3
White, Miss Laura	31 Dec 1877	Once a resident of Wilmington, now at "her southern home."	3

Alphabetical Order by Person listed			
Name Mentioned	Date	Subject	Scrapbook Page
White, Miss Minnie L.	Marriages, n.d.	Married at Middle Granville 10 Dec 1879 Edward W. Harringan of Comstocks. She is daughter of Geo. C. White of Middle Granville, and granddaughter of the late Peter Comstock of Port Kent.	11
White, Theodore H.	Marriage, n.d.	Married Flora C. Bliss 6 Aug 1878 at Wilmington's Congregational Parsonage by Rev. T. Watson. Groom lives at Keene Valley.	5
White, Mrs. Theodore	15 May 1881	From North Elba. Visiting at the John Bliss'.	20
White, Mr. And Mrs. Theodore	16 Dec 1878	From Keene. Attend church.	7
Wilkins, Albert	Obit, n.d.	His eldest son Charley aged 16, died by drowning 9 Jul 1878 in Wilmington.	4
Wilkins, Albert	10 Jul [1878]	His eldest son drowned. About same age as his sister, Jennie.	6
Wilkins, Albert	16 Dec 1878	Has a new shed.	7
Wilkins, Albert	19 Apr 1881	"Has drawn a pension of $750."	19

Alphabetical Order by Person listed			
Name Mentioned	Date	Subject	Scrapbook Page
Wilkins, Albert	21 Apr 1881	From Wilmington. His daughter Mrs. Frank Jordan, married for only a year, died. Funeral and burial 9 Apr 1881 in Wilmington. Services at Wilmington's Congregational Church.	20
Wilkins, Albert	21 Apr 1881	Drawn a pension of $750.	20
Wilkins, Albert	5 May 1881	Horse died.	20
Wilkins, Albert	21 Jul [1881]	Recites at village school closing ceremonies.	21
Wilkins, Mr. and Mrs. Albert	25 Jun 1879	Both injured by horse and carriage accident	10
Wilkins, Mr. and Mrs. Albert	1 Jul [1879]	"Slowly recovering from their accident."	10
Wilkins, Mr. and Mrs. Albert	10 Jul 1879	Have recovered from their injuries.	11
Wilkins, Alverdo	21 Jul [1881]	Recites (twice) at village school closing ceremonies.	21
Wilkins, Miss Amanda	18 Mar [1880]	From Montreal. Visiting friends.	14
Wilkins, Charley	Obit, n.d.	Aged 16 years, eldest son of Albert Wilkins died by drowning 9 Jul 1878 in Wilmington.	4
Wilkins, Carrie	21 Jul [1881]	Recites at village school closing ceremonies.	21
Wilkins, Frank	22 Mar 1878	Acted in play at Wilmington M.E. Church.	4
Wilkins, Frank	22 Oct 1879	Recited at M.E. Sunday School concert.	13

Alphabetical Order by Person listed

Name Mentioned	Date	Subject	Scrapbook Page
Wilkins, Frank	27 Feb 1880	Spoke at Wilmington's village school's graduation exercises.	14
Wilkins, Gilbert	18 Apr [1879]	Catches a yearling bear and offers for sale. He is son-in-law of Mr. M. Perry.	9
Wilkins, Guy	21 Jul [1881]	Recites at village school closing ceremonies.	21
[Wilkins], Miss Jennie	10 Jul [1878]	Has taken care of Albert Wilkins family since death of her mother.	6
Wilkins, Landin	23 Feb [1878]	Hurt his eye.	8
Wilkins, Landin	13 Jun [1878]	Family members have measles.	5
Wilkins, Landin	23 Jan [1879]	Building new house.	7
Wilkins, Landon	21 Apr 1881	Lost a valuable horse.	20
Wilkins, Mr. and Mrs. Landon	10 Dec 1880	Will have a "family Christmas tree" and entire family will gather.	[17]
Wilkins, Leander	27 Feb 1880	Read essay at Wilmington's village school's graduation exercises.	14
Wilkins, Onias	Marriages, n.d.	From Wilmington. Married Miss Rose Haselton of Wilmington in Wilmington by Rev. Thomas Watson at Congregational Parsonage 6 Dec 1879.	11
Wilkins, Mr. and Mrs. Onias	Births, n.d.	Son born to 29 Mar 1880 in Wilmington.	11
Wilkins, Mr. and Mrs. Onias	Births, n.d.	A daughter born to 11 Feb 1881 in Wilmington.	18

Alphabetical Order by Person listed			
Name Mentioned	Date	Subject	Scrapbook Page
Wilkins, Onlas	20 Apr 1878	Returned after a year from White Hills of New Hampshire.	4
William, S.G.	13 Dec 1877	Victim of break-in.	2
Williams, Mr.	7 Jan 1878	From Jay and now lives in Wilmington in Ira Storrs house on road leading to the Upper Forge.	3
Williams, Mrs.	12 Nov 1877	Has another narrow escape, returning from Keeseville.	1
Williams, Charles	12 Nov 1877	Nephew of Mrs. Sarah Ornsby, and of Elizabethtown.	1
Williams, G.G.	12 Nov 1877	Nephew of Mrs. Sarah Ornsby, and of Wilmington.	1
Williams, James	21 Jul [1881]	Recites at village school closing ceremonies.	21
Williams, Jimmie	27 Feb 1880	Won a spelling prize at Wilmington village school.	14
Williams, Jimmie	27 Feb 1880	Spoke at Wilmington's village school's graduation exercises.	14
Williams, Jimmie	9 Mar 1881	Recited at Wilmington village school closing exercises.	19
Williams, Milo	16 Apr [1879]	Has moved to Jay.	9
Williams, Mr. Milo	16 Dec 1878	Selling goods for Peru firm.	7
Williams, S.G.	21 May [1878]	Caring for his ill employee George Colby.	5

Alphabetical Order by Person listed			
Name Mentioned	Date	Subject	Scrapbook Page
Williams, S.G.	29 Aug 1878	Mrs. Daniel Ames and her son and daughter visit.	6
Williams, S.G.	30 Jul 1879	Defendant, with G.T. Hickok, in assault and battery case being tried at North Elba.	11
Williams, S.G.	13 Aug [1879]	Acquitted on charge of assault and battery in North Elba trial.	11
Williams, S.G.	24 Jun [1880]	Rev. John Mathews and family guests at, on their way to Lake Placid.	16
Williams, Mr. S.G.	1 Nov [1877]	Victim of theft.	1
Williams, Mr. S.G.	3 Apr 1878	Sold his flock of sheep.	4
Williams, Mr. S.G.	27 Dec [1878]	Theft of his oats and buckwheat.	7
Williams, Mr. And Mrs. S.G.	7 Jan 1878	Gave a New Years party for "little folks."	3
Wilson, James	29? Aug 1880	Moved into Amos Avery's house.	16
Wilson, Mrs. James	1 Jul [1879]	Quite sick, but recovering.	10
Wilson, Mr. and Mrs. James	Birth, n.d.	A daughter born to 8 Jan 1878 in Wilmington.	2
Winch, Asher	21 Jul [1881]	Recites at village school closing ceremonies.	21
Winch, C.	15 May 1881	House he formerly occupied, recently moved into by Mr. Bruce.	20
Winch, Cassius	21 May 1879	Has moved into Baldwin house.	10
Winch, Cassius	5 Jun 1879	He, and Edwin Hays, caught 60 lb of trout in 3 days "up the river."	10

Alphabetical Order by Person listed			
Name Mentioned	Date	Subject	Scrapbook Page
Winch, Cassius	16 Feb [1881]	Will repair Wilmington's bridge for $290 [Rescinded 2 Mar 1881 column.]	18
Winch, Cassius	15 May 1881	Bought house and lot from John Nye.	20
Winch, Fred	7 Jan 1878	Gave a well attended oyster New Years supper.	3
Winch, Fred	21 Apr 1880	Has moved onto Zach Lawrence farm.	15
Winch, Mr. and Mrs. Fred	Births, n.d.	A daughter born to 18 Jan 1880 in Wilmington.	13
Winch, Mrs. Ira	20 Nov [1877]	Quite ill.	1
Winch, Will	13 Dec 1877	Co-leader of theft ring.	2
Winch, Mrs. William	13 Feb 1878	Funeral services for on Monday.	3
Winters, Miss	8 Jul 1880	From Schuyler Falls. Visiting her sister, Mrs. Bosworth.	16
Winters, Miss Emma	30 Jul 1879	From Wilmington. Working at Stevens House, North Elba	11
Winters, Miss Emma	22 Oct 1879	Recited and sang at M.E. Sunday school concert.	13
Yaw, Mr. and Mrs. H.W.	Birth, n.d.	Son born to 30 Jun 1879 in East Franklin, VT.	8

Listing by Event

Event	Date	Description	Page
Accidents	25 Jun 1879	Two wheel rig accident; two people hurt.	10
Accidents	25 Jun 1879	Runaway horse and buggy, but no one hurt.	10
Accidents	1 Jul [1879]	Horse and wagon injure owner.	10
Agriculture	13 Jun [1878]	Frost and replanting.	5
Agriculture	26 Jun 1878	Crops flourishing: early potatoes in bloom; hay needs cutting.	6
Agriculture	10 Jul [1878]	Crops suffer from lack of rain; upland crops may fail.	6
Agriculture	13 Sept 1878	A second crop possible, especially of heavy clover.	7
Agriculture	26 Mar 1879	Fodder scarce.	9
Agriculture	16 Apr [1879]	Late planting.	9
Agriculture	24 Apr 1879	Spring farm work beginning.	9
Agriculture	5 Jun 1879	Potato bugs appear.	10
Agriculture	12 Jun 1879	Late frost harms fruit.	10
Agriculture	17 Jul 1879	Good hay crop.	11
Agriculture	30 Jul 1879	Haying bee.	11
Agriculture	6 Aug [1879]	Drought.	11
Agriculture	13 Aug [1879]	Drought lifted.	11
Agriculture	25 Sept 1879	Crop yields.	12

Listing by Event

Event	Date	Description	Page
Agriculture	25 Sept 1879	Threshing.	12
Agriculture	21 Apr 1880	Plowing and setting out fruit.	15
Agriculture	5 May 1880	Farmers are very busy.	15
Agriculture	5 May 1880	Potato bugs appear.	15
Agriculture	9 Jun 1880	Crops looking fine.	15
Agriculture	16 Jun 1880	A year for vermin.	16
Agriculture	24 Jun [1880]	Potatoes in bloom.	16
Agriculture	24 Jun [1880]	Looks like green peas and string beans.	16
Agriculture	24 Jun [1880]	Hay crop may be down.	16
Agriculture	8 Jul 1880	New potatoes, string beans as of 2nd; started to hay.	16
Agriculture	14 Jul 1880	Good crops.	16
Agriculture	7 Aug [1880]	Finished haying.	16
Agriculture	19 Apr 1881	Hay is getting scarce.	19
Agriculture	22 Jun [1881]	Long cold spell and report on crops (corn, potatoes, grain, and hay.)	20
Agriculture	12 Jul 1881	Some farmers now haying.	21
Agriculture	21 Jul [1881]	Cold June: poor apple harvest.	21
Agriculture	17 Aug [1881]	Mixed results on hay crop.	21
Annual school meeting	14 Oct [1880]	Election. Women do not attend.	[17]

Listing by Event

Event	Date	Description	Page
Bears	8 Apr [1879]	Fear of bears, and catching a yearling bear.	9
Bears	21 May 1879	"Quite a number [of bears] have been seen, and bait has been taken off the traps set to catch them."	10
Black Brook Catholic Church	23 Jan [1879]	Benefit for raises $50.	7
Bridge	9 Mar 1881	"The last contract for building our bridge was not strictly in accordance with the will of the people and has been thrown overboard." Rupert will not report anything more on subject until a bridge is actually built.	19
Bridge	19 Apr 1881	Bridge at last built.	19
Chick-a-dee	n.d. [between 9 Mar and 6 Apr 1881]	Passed through Wilmington last week.	19
Churches	3 Apr 1878	Three churches in Wilmington: evidently Congregational, Wesleyan Methodist (W.M.) and Methodist Episcopal (M.E.).	4
Churches	21 May 1879	Two churches in Wilmington: Congregational and M.E. have Sabbath Schools.	10
Churches	24 Jun [1880]	Two churches [as in 1879] in Wilmington.	16

Listing by Event

Event	Date	Description	Page
Churches		Schedule of meetings, etc. for both given.	
Commerce	7 Jul 1881	Timothy Jacquis is buying butter, eggs, and poultry for the hotels in Lake Placid.	20
Commerce	17 Aug [1881]	Buying fat cattle.	21
Congregational Church of Wilmington	15 Jan 1878	"Series of protracted meetings."	3
Congregational Church of Wilmington	15 May 1878	Sunday School reorganized.	5
Congregational Church of Wilmington	21 May [1878]	Has new library of Sunday School (SS) books.	10
Congregational Church of Wilmington	16 Jun 1880	SS organized. Rev. Thomas Watson engaged for another year.	16
Congregational Church of Wilmington	24 Jun [1880]	Schedules of services, etc.	16
Congregational Church of Wilmington	24 Nov [1880]	SS closed, in contrast to M.E. which will continue through Winter.	[17]
Congregational Church of Wilmington	Deaths, n.d.	M.E. Pastor officiates at funeral at Congregational Church.	18
Court session	12 Feb 1879	"Last Saturday the air was full of law suits, we believe no one was hurt."	8

Listing by Event			
Event	Date	Description	Page
Court session	5 Jun 1879	"Law suits all settled...," even though expensive for town.	10
Crime	22 Oct 1877	Selling apple trees under false pretenses.	1
Crime	1 Nov [1877]	Theft of meal, hens and rooster.	1
Crime	20 Nov [1877]	Theft of honey, hens, nails, and spikes.	1
Crime	26 Nov [1877]	Theft of Thanksgiving turkey, a hive and honey.	2
Crime	5 Dec 1877	Theft of grain and sheep.	2
Crime	13 Dec 1877	Gang of thieves with headquarters in house of ill fame. Arrest made or pending.	2
Crime	31 Dec 1877	Fatal stabbing at the Forks.	3
Crime	26 Jun 1878	Theft of a barrel of pork, but theft discovered.	6
Crime	26 Jun 1878	"A base outrage upon a little girl. Culprit indited, but flees."	6
Crime	26 Jun 1878	Wood shed stolen.	6
Crime	10 Jul [1878]	Store broken into, many goods stolen.	6
Crime	27 Dec [1878]	Hard times leads to crime.	7
Crime	15 Jan [1879]	House window broken.	7
Crime	23 Jan [1879]	List of items stolen, mainly grain.	7
Crime	12 Feb 1879	Thefts (corn and flour).	8

Listing by Event

Event	Date	Description	Page
Crime	13 Jan 1881	Prank. Theft of water pail and wood piled on highway.	18
Crow tax	9 Mar 1881	"The first crow tax was *cawed* for Thursday."	19
Deer Slayer	19 May 1880	Opposes a "ridiculous bill." A fellow town reporter?	15
Disease	20 Nov [1877]	Smallpox.	1
Disease	13 Jun [1878]	Measles.	5
Disease	12 Feb 1879	Bad colds.	8
Disease	17 Dec 1879	"Hard colds" and "croup."	13
Disease	18 Mar [1880]	Sore eyes and measles.	14
Disease	11 Apr 1880	Measles.	14
Disease	5 May 1880	Measles.	15
Disease	19 May 1880	Measles.	15
Disease	16 Jun 1880	Measles and horse distemper.	16
Disease	24 Nov [1880]	Much sickness.	[17]
Disclaimer	15 Jan 1878	Disclaimer about veracity of information.	3
Earthquake	6 Nov 1877	"No serious damage."	1
Earthquake	16 Apr [1879]	"A heavy shock."	9
Election	6 Nov 1877	Election. Women do not attend.	1

Listing by Event

Event	Date	Description	Page
Entertainment	12 Nov [1879]	"Last Saturday evening a large bonfire and the booming of cannon expressed the feelings of the people quite freely."	13
Entertainment	26 Nov 1879	Skating on frozen river "is the order of the day."	13
Entertainment	25 Jan 1880	Sleighing.	13
Entertainment	12 Mar 1879	"Surprise parties have been the rage all Winter."	8
Entertainment	12 Mar 1879	"Sugar parties come next."	
Entertainment	18 Mar 1880	No sleighing.	14
Entertainment	14 Oct [1880]	Cannonade.	[17]
Entertainment	13 Nov [1880]	Cannonade and political (Republican) victory	[17]
Entertainment		Celebration.	
Entertainment	10 Dec 1880	Skating and sliding.	[17]
Entertainment	13 Jan 1881	Sleighing.	18
Entertainment	27 Jan 1881	Fireman's ball held at Rogers Hall.	18
Entertainment	27 Jan 1881	Hounds used for hunting.	18
Entertainment	16 Apr 1881	Sugar parties.	19
Entertainment	21 Apr 1881	Sugar parties.	20
Fire	4 Jul [1878]	House burns. Family narrowly escapes.	6

Listing by Event

Event	Date	Description	Page
Fire	10 Dec 1879	Gristmill began to burn, but saved.	13
Fire	11 Apr 1880	Bridges over two kilns burn.	14
Fourth of July	4 Jul [1878]	Reflection upon the meaning of the 4th.	5
Fourth of July	10 Jul 1879	No public celebration at Wilmington.	11
Fourth of July	8 Jul 1880	Quiet celebration in Wilmington. Most from W. went to AuSable Forks for celebration.	16
Fourth of July	7 Jul 1881	"We" went to Keeseville for celebration.	20
Foxes	10 Dec 1880	10 turkeys in one flock taken.	[17]
Freedmen's Aid Society	6 Mar [1879]	Benefit collection for.	8
Garfield and Arthur Club	15 Sep 1880	One being formed at village school.	[17]
Hancock and English Club	15 Sept 1880	One to be formed in Markhamville.	[17]
Housecleaning	25 Apr 1878	"The ladies are...busy house cleaning."	5
Ice harvesting	15 Jan [1879]	Good harvest.	7
Industries	16 Dec 1878	Dam, gristmill, saw mill.	7
Industries	26 May 1880	Kilns on US side of AuSable River.	15
Industries	4 Aug 1881	Carriage shop.	21
Insect Infestations	25 Apr 1878	Colorado bug and potatoes.	5
Insect Infestations	13 Jun [1878]	Potato bugs.	5

Listing by Event

Event	Date	Description	Page
Insect Infestations	5 Jun 1879	Potato bugs arrive.	10
Iron bridge	16 Feb [1881]	"After close consultation among the officers and leading men of the town" it was decided against "an expensive iron bridge" and that the old one will be repaired.	18
Iron Works	2 Jan [1879]	"The forge is not running, and the bloomers think times are dull."	7
Iron Works	21 May 1879	"The forge is now running and business better." Evidently forge has major impact on local economy.	10
Iron Works	5 Jun 1879	"The forge is idle; we understand the bloomers have struck for higher wages."	10
Iron Works	12 Jun 1879	"The forge commenced running again Monday. The bloomers get fifty cents more on a ton."	10
Iron Works	9 Oct 1879	Forge is idle this week.	12
Iron Works	22 Oct 1879	Forge is idle at present.	13
Iron Works	12 Nov [1879]	Forge will start next Monday. New engine for separating ore taken to Keene.	13
Iron Works	10 Dec 1879	Forge running. Starts fire.	13

Listing by Event

Event	Date	Description	Page
Iron Works	25 Jan 1880	Forge is running steadily, as there is a good supply of wood.	13
Iron Works	13 Feb [1880]	Only two fires due to scarcity of coal.	14
Iron Works	27 Jan 1881	New kilns at North Elba.	18
Iron Works	23 Feb [1881]	Four fires running; lots of wood coming in.	18
Iron Works	2 Mar 1881	"The forge is idle owing to a proposed reduction of wages, which the bloomers do not propose to submit to."	18
Iron Works	9 Mar 1881	"The forge commenced running again...the bloomers having submitted to a reduction of fifty cents per ton."	19
Maple sugar	3 Apr 1878	Lots being made in town.	4
Mason family	10 Dec 1879	"The Mason Family exhibited at the W.M. Church."	13
M.E. Church in Wilmington	22 Oct 1877	End of Sabbath School exercises and celebration.	1
M.E. Church in Wilmington	20 Nov [1877]	Quarterly meeting.	1
M.E. Church in Wilmington	15 Jan 1878	Baptist minister from Jay preaches at.	3
M.E. Church in Wilmington	23 Jan 1878	M.E. and Presbyterian Churches hold combined meetings.	3
M.E. Church in Wilmington	26 Jun 1878	Baptism by sprinkling and immersion.	6

Listing by Event

Event	Date	Description	Page
M.E. Church in Wilmington	24 Aug 1878	Sunday School scholars picnic in Jay.	6
M.E. Church in Wilmington	6 Aug [1879]	Money raised for organ.	11
M.E. Church in Wilmington	25 Sept 1879	Sunday School joins in Union picnic with schools of Lower Jay, Upper Jay, and Keene.	12
M.E. Church in Wilmington	2 Oct 1879	Sunday School picnic deliberations.	12
M.E. Church in Wilmington	9 Oct 1879	Union picnic decided against and so held "at home"; described.	12
M.E. Church in Wilmington	9 Oct 1879	Sunday School concert.	12
M.E. Church in Wilmington	22 Oct 1879	Detailed description of Sunday School concert.	13
M.E. Church in Wilmington	25 Jan 1880	Pastor holding a "series of meetings."	13
M.E. Church in Wilmington	13 Feb [1880]	Quarterly meeting.	14
M.E. Church in Wilmington	13 Feb [1880]	Pastor holding a series of meetings.	14
M.E. Church in Wilmington	18 Mar [1880]	Protracted effort is a success.	14
M.E. Church in Wilmington	30 Mar 1880	3 baptized, 3 received on probation, 1 taken in full communion.	14
M.E. Church in Wilmington	24 Jun [1880]	Schedule for several church services and meetings given.	16
M.E. Church in Wilmington	29? Aug [1880]	Quarterly meeting.	16

Listing by Event

Event	Date	Description	Page
M.E. Church in Wilmington	24 Nov [1880]	Sabbath School to continue through Winter [compared to Congregational Sunday School which closed 3 weeks ago.]	[17]
M.E. Church in Wilmington	15 May 1881	Sabbath School reorganized.	20
M.E. Church in Wilmington	9 Mar 1881	"Young people" met to establish a group to organize "an exhibition for the purpose of purchasing an organ stool and chandeliers for the church."	19
M.E. Church Xmas Program	26 Nov 1879	Outline [compare with SS concert 22 Oct 1879.]	13
M.E. Church Xmas Program	10 Dec 1879	Arrangements made to erect Xmas tree.	13
M.E. Church Xmas Program	25 Dec [1879]	Comments on.	13
M.E. Church Xmas Program	10 Dec 1880	Will be Xmas tree on Xmas eve.	[17]
Moonshining and bootlegging	3 Apr 1878	Temperance laws being violated.	4
Pensions	18 Mar [1880]	"Quite a number" are getting pensions.	14
Peru Peddler	10 Jul [1878]	Late for church.	6
Politics	6 Mar [1879]	Rupert supports Democrats.	8
Politics	1 Apr [1879]	Wilmington not fertile ground for Greenback Party.	9
Politics	27 Feb 1880	Caucus night.	14

Listing by Event			
Event	Date	Description	Page
Politics	29? Aug 1880	Little activity "for either candidate."	16
Politics	15 Sept 1880	Political clubs founded.	[17]
Politics	22 Sept 1880	Several items (…meetings.)	[17]
Politics	4 Nov [1880]	Republican victory in Wilmington.	[17]
Politics	22 Sept 1880	Republicans meeting in Wilmington and Democrats in Markhamville.	[17]
Politics	4 Nov [1880]	"The great Republican victory in Wilmington" implies that votes "sold."	[17]
Politics	13 Nov [1880]	Republican victory celebration.	[17]
Politics	2 Mar 1881	"A stump ticket was gotten up on Monday, but the full caucus ticket was elected."	18
Postal service	30 Jul 1879	Took 6 days for a letter to arrive from Keeseville. Evidently an unusually long delay.	11
Presbyterian Church	23 Jan 1878	Joint meeting with M.E.	3
Prostitution	13 Dec 1877	House of "ill fame" and gang of thieves.	2
Prostitution	15 May 1878	Theft ring "at last broken up."	5
Religion	25 Jun 1879	Amusing religious story.	10

Listing by Event			
Event	Date	Description	Page
Religion	26 Aug 1879	Quite a number "from Wilmington attending a camp meeting in Jay."	12
Roads	12 Jun 1879	"The road leading over the mountain is being improved."	10
Roads	24 Jun [1880]	Roads being repaired.	16
Roads	27 Jan 1881	Keeping roads passable.	18
Rogers Kilns	23 Dec 1880	So few scholars, that no school will be held there this Winter.	[17]
Rupert's ID	15 May [1878]	"A visit from Mr. And Mrs. L.F. Mace was enjoyed by us last week."	5
Rupert's ID	15 May [1878]	"We take this opportunity of recommending…L.F. Mace's Vegetable Lung Remedy."	5
Rupert's ID	27 Dec [1878]	"We acknowledge the receit of a very pretty Christmas gift from Winooski Falls, VT."	7
Rupert's ID	23 Jan [1879]	"We had the pleasure of attending.." benefit for Catholic Church at Black brook.	7
Rupert's ID	n.d.	News from VT and PQ (Berkshire Center, VT)	0
Rupert's ID	n.d.	News from VT and PQ (St. Armond, PQ)	4
Rupert's ID	n.d.	News from VT and PQ (East Franklin, VT)	6

Listing by Event

Event	Date	Description	Page
Rupert's ID	n.d.	News from VT and PQ (East Franklin, VT)	8
Rupert's ID	23 Feb [1879]	"Being personally acquainted with..."	8
Rupert's ID	6 Mar [1879]	Herbert E. Hinds visits "us."	8
Rupert's ID	24 Apr 1879	"Choir meeting Sat. afternoon at four" but doesn't indicate which church! Obviously her readers knew it is M.E.	9
Rupert's ID	30 Apr [1879]	Reports death of Wesley Galusha.	9
Rupert's ID	9 May 1879	"Everyone is anxious to hear the new minister next Sabbath."	9
Rupert's ID	21 May 1879	"We enjoyed a pleasant call from...[E.S. Kemp]"	10
Rupert's ID	5 Jun 1879	"We enjoyed a pleasant call from...[E.S. Kemp]"	10
Rupert's ID	21 May 1879	"Our new pastor, the Rev. McKernan."	10
Rupert's ID	21 May and 5 Jun 1879	"Mr. Printor" made error, D.S. Knapp really is E.S. Kemp.	10
Rupert's ID	5 Jun 1879	Visited E.S. Kemp "of Adirondack House at the Forks."	10
Rupert's ID	25 Jun 1879	"Bro. McKernan."	10
Rupert's ID	25 Jun 1879	"We enjoyed a pleasant call from Mr. J Washer, of Clintonville an agent for the Meadow King Mowing Machine."	10

Listing by Event

Event	Date	Description	Page
Rupert's ID	1 Jul [1879]	"We enjoyed a pleasant visit from...Master Herbert Hinds."	10
Rupert's ID	1 Jul [1879]	"Mr. And Mrs. E.S. Kemp...called to-day."	10
Rupert's ID	30 Jul 1879	"We are enjoying a pleasant visit from Mrs. E.S. Kemp and Master Frankie."	11
Rupert's ID	6 Aug [1879]	"We enjoyed a pleasant call from Dr. J. Sanford of Castleton, VT and A. Mace of AuSable."	11
Rupert's ID	26 Aug 1879	She is a member of the M.E. Church's choir.	12
Rupert's ID	26 Aug 1879	"We enjoyed a pleasant call from W. Lansing of Keeseville."	12
Rupert's ID	2 Oct 1879	"Rutland papers received with pleasure. Many thanks."	12
Rupert's ID	26 Nov 1879	Will spend Thanksgiving at Forks.	13
Rupert's ID	12 Nov 1879	Pays a lot of attention to who is getting teaching posts.	13
Rupert's ID	26 Nov 1879	Pays a lot of attention to who is getting teaching posts.	13
Rupert's ID	10 Dec 1879	Henry Hinds lost a valuable cow.	13
Rupert's ID	25 Jan 1880	Visit of Capt. A.L. Galusha to John Hinds.	13
Rupert's ID	11 Apr 1880	John Hinds' new organ (elaborate description).	14

Listing by Event

Event	Date	Description	Page
Rupert's ID	21 Apr 1880	Mentions a Richard Hinds, battery salesman.	15
Rupert's ID	n.d.	Unusually detailed death announcement for son of E.S. Kemp.	15
Rupert's ID	26 May 1880	E.S. Kemp visit to J. Hinds'.	15
Rupert's ID	26 May 1880	"Our Sutton P.Q. correspondent reports."	15
Rupert's ID	16 Jun 1880	"We are sorry to learn of the serious illness of Mrs. P.V. Hewitt."	16
Rupert's ID	24 Jun [1880]	"We enjoyed a pleasant call from Mrs. C.F. Nye of Keene."	16
Rupert's ID	13 Aug 1880	"We attended" funeral of Isaac Owen.	16
Rupert's ID	14 Oct [1880]	Hon. Asa Frary of Sutton, PQ visits.	[17]
Rupert's ID	4 Nov [1880]	"We enjoyed...call from Mr. And Mrs. Leroy Gaskill of Clintonville." Is Mrs. "Osceola"?	[17]
Rupert's ID	13 Nov [1880]	Long obit for Mrs. Kemp.	[17]
Rupert's ID	24 Nov [1880]	Visit of Miss Hattie Wells of Frelightsburg P.Q.	[17]
Rupert's ID	21 Apr 1881	Mrs. E.S. Kemp is John Hinds' guest.	20
Rupert's ID	5 May 1881	Rev. E.J. Kernan will continue as "our pastor."	20
Rupert's ID	7 Jul 1881	"We enjoyed the Fourth at Keeseville."	20

Listing by Event

Event	Date	Description	Page
Rupert's ID	15 May 1881	"We were agreeably surprised by..." "visit of Mr. and Mrs. E.S. Kemp of AuSable Forks and Mr. and Mrs. A.W. Galusha of Ogdensburg.	20
Rupert's ID	22 Jun [1881]	"We attended the funeral of Miss Mary O'Neil."	20
Rupert's ID	14 Aug [1881]	Mrs. S.A. Beardsley M.D., "our old and esteemed friend."	21
Rupert, misc.	2 Jan [1879]	Evidently subscribes to *Godey's Lady's Book*. See also 27 Jan 1881, p.18.	7
Rupert, misc.	6 Mar [1879]	Describes election of Democrats at town meeting as "This is unexpected, rich, and rare for this place."	8
Rupert, misc.	24 Apr 1879	Made another mistake.	9
Rupert, misc.	26 Nov 1879	"News is scarce."	13
Rupert, misc.	17 Dec 1879	Hopes Editor will forgive her many mistakes and "we hope in the future to have more time to devote to your interesting paper."	13
Rupert, misc.	25 Jan 1880	"Our time has been limited and items of interest scarce." No column from Dec until 25 Jan.	13

Listing by Event

Event	Date	Description	Page
Rupert, misc.	5 May 1880	Mr. Editor, you forgot to mention the Wilmington Jewhangdoodle Gossiper.	15
Rupert, misc.	26 May 1880	Evidently does not support Women's Rights---refers to "the fastidious state of the coming women man."	19
Rupert, misc.	9 Jun 1880	"Well, Mr. Editor. It seems we can't vote for Grant this year. Too bad isn't it?"	15
Rupert, misc.	24 Jun [1880]	"Hope Ed and Phebe will call again, we just enjoyed it."	16
Rupert, misc.	14 Oct [1880]	"To-night the old cannon is booming forth it's greeting to Indiana and Ohio."	[17]
Rupert, misc.	14 Oct [1880]	Women should not be at the annual school meeting.	[17]
Rupert, misc.	23 Feb [1881]	"A number of our young people spent the 22nd in North Elba."	18
Rupert?	27 Jan 1881	An "AuSable Forks" column for 27 Jan 1881, on p.18, is included in scrapbook, and signed "VISITOR." Must be Ruperts column.	18
Rupert's poetry	25 Mar 1878	On death of a child.	4
Rupert's poetry	4 Jul 1878	On suddenly being poor.	6

Listing by Event

Event	Date	Description	Page
Rupert's poetry	6 Mar 1879	Gold and unfolding of seasons.	8
Rupert's poetry	1 Jul [1879]	On death of a child.	10
Rupert's poetry	23 Feb [1881]	Types of news.	18
Rupert's poetry	21 Apr 1881	On death; and on Spring.	20
Sabbath Schools	12 Mar 1879	Time to "reorganize."	8
Sabbath Schools	21 May 1879	"Are now organized."	10
Sabbath Schools	8 Jul 1880	"The Sabbath Schools are both in a flourishing condition."	16
Sabbath quarterly meeting	17 Aug [1881]	Held at Wilmington.	21
Sabbath Schools picnic	13 Sept 1878	Detailed description of.	7
School closing	27 Feb 1880	Closing exercises.	14
School closing	7 Aug [1880]	Closing exercises.	16
School closing	9 Mar 1881	Closing exercises.	19
School closing	21 Jul 1881	Closing exercises.	21
School teachers	2 Mar 1881	"School maams are as thick as musquitoes."	18
Singing schools	16 Dec 1878	Are a success.	7
Singing schools	12 Feb 1879	They still flourish.	8
Singing schools	16 Apr [1879]	They close.	9
Stevens House of North Elba/Lake Placid	17 Jul 1879	Ed Bliss employed by J. Stevens of North Elba at hotel.	11

Listing by Event

Event	Date	Description	Page
Stevens House of North Elba/Lake Placid	17 Jul 1879	Travelers plan to visit Stevens House.	11
Stevens House of North Elba/Lake Placid	30 Jul 1879	2 young unmarried women employed at.	11
Stevens House of North Elba/Lake Placid	6 Aug [1879]	2 young unmarried women employed at.	11
Stevens House of North Elba/Lake Placid	6 Aug [1879]	James Bliss takes his team to and is staging for.	11
Stevens House of North Elba/Lake Placid	6 Aug [1879]	School closes. Teacher off to.	11
Stevens House of North Elba/Lake Placid	26 Aug 1879	4 of Bliss family at.	12
Stevens House of North Elba/Lake Placid	7 Aug [1880]	Edmond Bliss staging for.	16
Storrs House	26 Aug 1878	A Wilmington hotel.	12
Storrs House	22 Sept 1880	Flying a Garfield and Arthur flag.	[17]
Storrs House	24 Nov [1880]	Purchase a new stage.	[17]
Sunday School picnic	15 Sept 1880	Annual one combines Wilmington and Markhamville	[17]
Sunday School picnic	22 Sept 1880	Description of. Note: combines both M.E. and Congregational Churches! Evidently because of weather Markhamville's held separately.	[17]
Taxes	19 Dec 1877	"Are unusually high."	2

Listing by Event			
Event	Date	Description	Page
Taxes	19 Jun [1878]	Assessment.	5
Taxes	12 Mar 1879	Satire on.	8
Taxes	16 Apr 1879	Crow tax.	9
Taxes	22 Jun [1881]	Disapproves of increase in tax.	20
Teaching institute	8 Jul 1880	"Our teachers all attended the Institute at Elizabethtown."	16
Temperance	1 Mar 1878	"The tidal wave of Temperance."	4
Temperance	3 Apr 1878	Temperance laws broken.	4
Temperance	25 Dec [1879]	Rum drinkers at church Xmas celebrations.	13
Temperance	16 Feb [1881]	A long statement on temperance, religion, and slavery.	18
Tourism	10 Jul 1879	Tour route.	11
Tourism	6 Aug [1879]	Tour routes.	11
Tourism	26 Aug 1879	Tour route.	12
Tourism	26 Aug 1879	Attraction of Wilmington.	12
Tourism	7 Jul 1881	How Wilmington affected by Lake Placid.	20
Tourism	15 May 1881	Notch House.	20
Town house	26 May 1880	Building of coupled to women's issues.	15
Town house	24 Jun [1880]	Building of not yet been settled.	16
Town house	23 Dec 1880	Purchased Hall's store building for.	[17]

Listing by Event

Event	Date	Description	Page
Town house	2 Mar 1881	Not yet completed.	18
Town meeting	6 Mar [1879]	"Was rather stormy." 3 Democrats elected. See also 2 Mar 1881.	8
Unemployment	16 Dec 1878	Many need work.	7
Unemployment	27 Dec [1878]	Hard times leads to crime.	7
The Valley	10 Dec 1879	"Quite a number of our townsmen have been at the Valley this week.	13
Weather	22 Oct 1877	Frost and it remains cool.	1
Weather	6 Nov 1877	Mountains are covered with snow.	1
Weather	20 Nov [1877]	Cold, windy, and snow flies.	1
Weather	19 Dec 1877	Weather lovely, but a little cooler.	2
Weather	31 Dec 1877	No snow, but frost. River frozen over.	3
Weather	7 Jan 1878	Snow at last.	3
Weather	15 Jan 1878	Weather warm and pleasant.	3
Weather	23 Jan 1878	January thaw left ground bare.	3
Weather	13 Feb 1878	Plenty of snow. A strong Southwester.	3
Weather	1 Mar 1878	Little snow. Lots of ice. Thaw, then freezing.	4
Weather	22 Mar 1878	March weather: cold and blustering.	4
Weather	25 Mar 1878	Snow all gone. Lots of mud. Lovely Spring weather.	4

Listing by Event

Event	Date	Description	Page
Weather	3 Apr 1878	Glorious Spring weather.	4
Weather	20 Apr 1878	Spring and no danger of snow.	4
Weather	25 Apr 1878	An early Spring.	5
Weather	13 Jun [1878]	Cool weather.	5
Weather	10 Jul [1878]	A lack of rain.	6
Weather	16 Dec 1878	Freshet and damage.	7
Weather	16 Dec 1878	Quite cold...	7
Weather	27 Dec 1878	Lots of snow. Horrible wind. No sleighing or wagoning	7
Weather	2 Jan [1879]	Blow over. Good sleighing.	7
Weather	15 Jan [1879]	Extremely cold.	7
Weather	23 Jan [1879]	Jan. thaw has turned cold.	7
Weather	12 Feb 1879	Weather is very unsettled.	8
Weather	6 Mar [1879]	Cold and blustering.	8
Weather	18 Mar [1879]	Snow and good sleighing.	8
Weather	26 Mar 1879	8 inches of snow, but melting.	9
Weather	1 Apr [1879]	Cold and stormy.	8
Weather	16 Apr [1879]	A foot of snow. Frost still reigns.	8
Weather	24 Apr 1879	Still plenty of snow.	9
Weather	21 May 1879	A shower.	10

Listing by Event

Event	Date	Description	Page
Weather	29 May 1879	Rain needed. Slight frosts.	10
Weather	5 Jun 1879	Rain at last.	10
Weather	12 Jun 1879	Late frosts.	10
Weather	6 Aug [1879]	Rain needed. A terrible wind.	11
Weather	13 Aug [1879]	Much needed rain.	11
Weather	25 Sept 1879	A slight scale of ice on standing water.	12
Weather	12 Nov [1879]	An abundance of rain	13
Weather	26 Nov 1879	River is frozen over.	13
Weather	10 Dec 1879	"A heavy wind."	13
Weather	25 Jan 1880	Sleighing snow nearly all gone.	13
Weather	4 Feb [1880]	A foot of snow fell.	13
Weather	13 Feb [1880]	Snow all gone except for a few drifts.	14
Weather	18 Mar [1880]	No snow yet this month, and little for winter.	14
Weather	21 Apr 1880	Farmers are plowing and setting out fruit.	15
Weather	5 May 1880	Extremely warm.	15
Weather	12 May [1880]	Heavy wind.	15
Weather	19 May 1880	Spring.	15
Weather	24 Jun [1880]	Need rain.	16
Weather	4 Nov [1880]	Unexpected frost.	[17]

Listing by Event

Event	Date	Description	Page
Weather	10 Dec 1880	Snow gone, breeze, ice. Three times.	[17]
Weather	27 Jan 1881	Show and breeze.	18
Weather	23 Feb [1881]	Thaw and very cold.	18
Weather	2 Mar 1881	March in like a lion.	18
Weather	6 Apr 1881	Windy, late thaw.	19
Weather	21 Apr 1881	Spring.	20
Weather	22 Jun [1881]	Long cold spell.	20
Weather	21 Jul [1881]	Cold weather in June.	21
Wedding Anniversary Celebration	16 Dec 1878	Mr. and Mrs. H.J. Huntington's tenth described.	7
Wedding Anniversary Celebration	10 Dec 1879	Mr. and Mrs. David Hays' tenth briefly described.	13
Wesleyan Methodist in Wilmington	3 Apr 1878	Not to be confused with M.E.	4
Wesleyan Methodist in Wilmington	10 Dec 1879	The "Mason Family exhibited at."	13
Whiteface, ascents of	17 Jul 1878	"Parties are beginning to make the ascent of old Whiteface."	11
Whiteface, ascents of	4 Sept 1879	Party of 8 from Markhamville ascended.	12
Women's Rights Day	26 May 1880	To be celebrated?	15
Women's Rights Day	17 Jun [1881]	Approves of a woman as Superintendent of SS.	20

Listing by Event

Event	Date	Description	Page
Women are source of news.	25 Apr 1878	Rupert's columns depend on.	5
Wood jobs	12 Nov [1879]	"Wood jobs, chopping and coaling, are the chief topics of interest at present."	13
Wood jobs	25 Jan 1880	Large quantities used for forge.	13
Wood jobs	4 Feb [1880]	Snow helps wood jobbers.	13
Wood jobs	13 Feb [1880]	Scarcity of coal.	13
Wood jobs	18 Mar [1880]	Scarcity of snow ruins some wood jobbers.	14
Wood jobs	28 Apr [1880]	Large number of men driving cordwood down river.	15
Wood jobs	5 May 1880	Quite a lot of wood has come down river.	15
Wood jobs	12 May [1880]	Some 800 cords of wood in river.	15
Wood jobs	19 May 1880	Coal as a substitute for wood?	15
Wood jobs	16 Jun 1880	Coal as a substitute for wood?	16
Wood jobs	23 Dec 1880	Several teams headed for lumber woods at Brighton.	[17]
Wood jobs	23 Feb [1881]	Lots of wood being drawn in to feed forge fires.	18

ABOUT THE AUTHORS

HAROLD HINDS, JR., Ph.D. and Distinguished Research Professor of History, the University of Minnesota, Morris, teaches a wide variety of history courses, including one on genealogy and personal family history. He has lectured extensively, from locally to internationally, and has delivered several key-note addresses; in addition to the Wilmington series, published four monographs, edited eighteen collections of scholarly essays, and published more than forty articles in genealogical and professional history journals; and is a member of numerous local, regional, and national history and genealogy organizations. He previously served as a Director-at-Large of the National Genealogical Society, and currently serves as consulting editor of *Minnesota Genealogist*, and as program chair of the West Central (Minnesota) Family History Association. His current research focuses on genealogical and historical methods for conducting personal family history, New York's Adirondacks, and Kentucky's Appalachia.

TINA DIDRECKSON, B.A., History, was a recipient of the prestigious 2003 Scholar of the College award from the University of Minnesota, Morris, prior to her graduation in 2003 with distinction. She was also twice the recipient of the BOS Research Fellowship Award. She is a technical assistant, freelance research consultant and an aspiring professional genealogist. Ms. Didreckson has presented lectures at the Minnesota Genealogical Society and at the 2003 Ohio Genealogical Society's *200 Years of Heritage* conference as well as the Steven's County (Minnesota) Genealogical Society. She is currently the coordinator of the West Central Family History Association and Staff Genealogist for the Stevens County Historical Society & Museum in Morris, Minnesota. Her current research focus is the Northern Plains states of South and North Dakota, Wyoming and Montana.

Other books by Harold E. Hinds, Jr. and Tina M. Didreckson:

Town of Wilmington, Essex County, New York Transcribed Serial Records
Volume 1: Wilmington Town Ledger, 1821–1865 (Cattle Earmarks, 1820s–1884)
Volume 2: 1850 U.S. Census Schedules and 1855 New York Census Schedules

Volume 3: 1860 Federal Population Census & Schedules, 1862 Wilmington Military Census Schedules, 1865 New York Population & Census Schedules, 1865 Wilmington Military Census Schedules

Volume 4: 1870 Federal Population Census & Schedules, 1870 Wilmington Mortality Schedules, 1875 New York Population Census & Schedules, 1875 Wilmington Mortality Schedules

Volume 5: 1830 U.S. Population Census; 1835 Statistical Summary; 1840 U.S. Population Census; 1845 Statistical Summary; 1847–1849 Birth, Death and Marriage Census; 1880 U.S. Population Census and Misc. Schedules; 1890 U.S. Military Census; 1892 N.Y. State Census
Tina M. Didreckson and Harold E. Hinds, Jr.

Volume 6: Wilmington Cemetery Records, 1804–2003
Harold E. Hinds, Jr., Tina M. Didreckson, Nancy Cressey and Robert Cressey

Volume 7: Emma Hinds' Scrapbook, 1877–1881
Harold E. Hinds, Jr., Tina Didreckson, and Janet Pederson

Volume 8: Dr. E. A. Robinson's Receipt Book, 1881–1882
Harold E. Hinds, Jr., Tina M. Didreckson and Janet Pederson

Volume 9: Wilmington School Records, 1822–1900
Harold E. Hinds, Jr. and Tina M. Didreckson

Volume 10: Tax Assessment Records, 1850–1869
Harold E. Hinds, Jr., Tina M. Didreckson and Erika Paulson

Volume 11: Tax Assessment Records, 1871–1890
Harold E. Hinds, Jr., Tina M. Didreckson and Erika Paulson

Volume 12: Tax Assessment Records, 1891–1900
Harold E. Hinds, Jr., Tina M. Didreckson and Erika Paulson

Volume 13: Wilmington Voting Records, 1860–1900
Harold Hinds, Jr., Tina M. Didreckson and Erika Paulson

CD: *Volume 14, 15 and 16: Wilmington General Store, 1852–1854*
Harold E. Hinds, Jr., Tina M. Didreckson and Joseph L. Swartz, Jr. with Sarah Coleman, Tami Jensen and Matthew H. Ottinger

Volume 17: Wilmington Church Records
Harold E. Hinds, Jr., Miranda K. Tjaden, and Tina M. Didreckson

Volume 18: Wilmington Newspaper Transcriptions, 1831–1889
Harold E. Hinds, Jr. and Tina M. Didreckson
with Escillia Allen, Ashley Deering, Ashia Girard,
Miranda Tjaden, Jeffrey A. Wencl and Alissa Melberg

Volume 19: Wilmington Newspaper Transcriptions, 1890–1900
Harold E. Hinds, Jr. and Tina M. Didreckson
with Escillia Allen, Ashley Deering, Ashia Girard,
Miranda Tjaden, Jeffrey A. Wencl and Alissa Melberg

Volume 21: Haselton, Blacksmith Ledger
Harold E. Hinds, Jr. and Tina M. Didreckson
with Ashley M. Deering and Miranda K. Tjaden

www.ingramcontent.com/pod-product-compliance
Lightning Source LLC
Chambersburg PA
CBHW072151160426
43197CB00012B/2331